Parallel Universes:

A Love Story Transcending

Death

By L. Shannon Andersen, LMHC

Sacred Escapes Publishing, Hammock, Florida

ISBN 0-9817894-3

Scared Escapes Publishing

www.TheMagdaleneAwakening.com

Dedicated to Pancho

Acknowledgements

Thanks to my children, Treve and Melissa. Thanks to my sister and best friends; Lissa, Beth, and Debbie. Thanks to my co-workers from Hospice of Volusia/Flagler in Florida. Thanks, especially, to Dale and Helen, the nurse and social worker for all they did to care for my husband.
Finally, thanks to editor Fred Welter, and Lynn Williams.

Preface

This is a story about death, the truest mystery in life. It is also a story about what happens following the loss of a loved one and the journey through the grief process. Death happens every day but I wanted proof consciousness survives. I wanted to be taught about death. When my husband was dying, I asked him if we could attempt to write a book using After Death Communication (ADCs). Both of us were familiar with synchronicities as defined by Carl Jung i.e.: meaningful reoccurring coincidences. Together we had both seen and recognized After Death Communications as defined by Bill Guggenheim co-author of *Hello from Heaven*. We did not know for sure we would be able to continue communication after he died. Neither he, nor I, was psychic. We were not sure how it might work but we parted open to possibilities. I was left behind to tell our story while he was freed to fly.

Our story is about the experiences we had before and after his death. It is about the signs he provided i.e.: signs like rainbows and hawks and synchronicities like seeing his name written across a wall in Peru. The story includes some of the important things I learned working as a hospice bereavement counselor while listening to people grieve in my daily job. The feelings and emotions of others accompanied my own as I struggled with my husband's dying process and ultimate death. I recorded my labor through my unique grief process with its familiar twists and spirals.

During the last 10 years working with hospice, I studied research done by doctors like Dr. Raymond Moody who completed over 45 years of study of the Near Death Experience (NDE) and others like Dr. Melvin Morris who exclusively studied the Near Death Experiences of children. My personal style of grief support encouraged an open-ended wonder, allowing my clients to consider the possibility that their loved one's consciousness survived the death of the body. Perhaps the dead could reach us from their new form of consciousness. Pancho provided me with all the evidence I needed to believe.

Table of Contents

AUTHOR'S NOTE

My husband died. My friend/brother/lover/partner left my side. Our children grieved the father they loved. This true tale I lay before you is a story of grief and exploration. What do you call it when a life at any age is taken by cancer? What happens following the death of a loved one? What felt like an unfair tragedy is not unusual. It happens every day to thousands of people, but the experience of death is unique to the individuals and the families living through it.

During the time leading up to a predicted death, the world usually shrinks down to a few people. In our case and like many others it included a hospice team to whom I owe so much. I was a part of that team for many years working as a grief counselor. In my work with hospice, I took the hand of the bereaved when their loved one died and walked beside them for as long as they needed me. I supported them and taught them about normal grief.

Because of my profession, I knew people survived grief. I had been a witness to their recovery over the last twelve years of my career. I would assure my bereavement clients they would survive. I could say with great confidence, *YOU WILL MAKE IT THROUGH THIS. I know because I have helped hundreds of people and they all do.* Therefore, when I faced the death of my own spouse and the grief that followed, I was well prepared.

Chapter One
William Clark "Pancho" Andersen

Pancho Andersen carried his own brand. There was no other like him. We could not have been more different. I was from a southern family, born and raised in Florida with my roots in North Carolina. I was brought up in the Methodist church with attendance every Sunday morning of my youth. His mother was born in Massachusetts and raised in Ohio. She married an emigrant from Denmark, who grew up in Brooklyn. Pancho's' New Yorker dad was genteel, belonged to the country club, played golf and read all the great works of literature. My father, youngest of nine from Hendersonville, North Carolina, was a hard working contractor who used his hands and could do anything.

My parents were Democrats, and his parents were Republican. My parents had a high school education, both his had graduated from college, the Miami University of Ohio. We, however, were both Florida born and for the most part Florida raised. Pancho had a Texan flair. We both loved horses and raised our own. Our first date was to a rodeo.

I could not figure out where Pancho got his southern drawl. Not from his family, that was for sure. Pancho spent his middle school years growing up in Richardson, Texas, outside Dallas. There he learned to love horses and caught his cowboy accent. He worked on a ranch and learned about real life from his boss, TD Sterns. TD ran a string of over a hundred rental horses. TD told great stories. Pancho took on the skill of storytelling and added a flavor of his own. He could entertain me for hours. During our last trip together to Nova Scotia, when he knew he did not have long to live, again he told me the story of growing up in Texas. I loved listening to his stories.

I met Pancho Andersen in Atlantic Beach, Florida where he grew up after returning from Texas. I was 20 and he was a year older. He had become a surfer, even president of the Utica surf club, a true honor of that time. Pancho worked in Mayport for Matt Rowland at the tiny fishing village near the large Naval Base not far from his home. He loved the water in every way: to surf, to fish. You rarely found Pancho far from water or with shoes. He was just a flip-flop, T-shirt, blue jeans kind of guy. It did not matter how many Brooks Brothers golf shirts his Mom gave him. She supplied all of his 'proper attire' throughout his life, from sport coats to boat shoes. Pancho was a rebel. His father was still wearing a crew cut and a skinny tie the first time I met him in 1973. Pancho's hair was long, blond like corn silk, and I am sure he did not own a tie. He would concede and dress up on Sunday for dinner at his parents' house, holidays, and special occasions. 'Proper attire' was shed at the first opportunity.

Pancho did not care to impress anyone with material things. I had grown up in a middle class home and enamored by his parents' life style. I fell in love with his family as much as I did with Pancho. Education was important to me because my parents were not college graduates. Pancho only went to college because his parents insisted and then only studied what he loved: Marine Biology. He went to Jacksonville University, but he never completed his degree. His real university was the world and in 1973, he began to educate me about a world I never knew.

Chapter Two:
Pancho's World

I had been taken to church, but Pancho taught me where God lived, in nature. I fell in love with Pancho when I first laid eyes on him. It was at a boyfriend's beach house. I bumped into him as he turned the hall corner, his hair bleached white from sun and surf, ragged jeans and a shirt with a tear on the pocket. He always wore Ray Bans that covered his blue eyes. The second time I met him I lifted the sunglasses in a rather bold move to check out those eyes. It was not long before he completely had my heart. When we went on a double date, Pancho in front with his date, I in back with mine, he reached his left hand around the seat to seek out my hand to hold. When he let me drive his brother's MG, he stopped at the corner of 3rd and 12th St. in Atlantic Beach and asked if he could kiss me.

That was it. There was no looking back. During those early years, I followed him like a puppy, even through the woods. I almost stepped on a moccasin as we waded through knee-deep marsh grass. I soon found myself covered by tiny seed ticks that sent me running back to the car to strip down to nothing. I sat up in a tree stand where I was directed to sit very still so as not to scare the deer or wild hogs, even though I was being eaten alive by mosquitoes. Thank goodness nothing walked by me.

With Pancho, I watched sunrises and the most precious thing he gave me was the moon. He taught me about the full moon rising over the ocean every month at sunset and together we watched a thousand moonrises. We were children of the 50s, teenagers in the 60s and lovers in the 70's. During our first years together, we hung out at Pete's Bar in Atlantic Beach and the Spectrum Disco Club. We traveled together to Puerto Rico and the Virgin Islands, England, France, Spain and Gibraltar, Morocco and North Africa. He proposed in Nice in a hotel overlooking the Mediterranean. We were together for five years and married in 1978 in a double wedding with Dean, his brother, in a Methodist Church in Jacksonville. In our early lives, we enjoyed freedom and fun. We gave the best parties, as many of our old friends can testify. We gave that all up in the 80s in order to raise a pair of amazing children. Now I know the real reason I married Pancho and the reason we stayed married for 34 years was due to those two amazing, beautiful kids. I knew he would father beautiful children.

The 90's were years of building his business in Mariculture. He cultivated clams from state leased marshlands. He got to work next to manatees and under eagles. He was strong from hard work, and after being diagnosed with stage four cancer in 2003, he made a pledge to surf and fish every day of his life. He took a fishing rod on his boat so on the way to work he'd have a chance to cast or troll on the way to his state leased marsh land located on the Matanzas River south of St. Augustine near Devil's Elbow. He was most comfortable in a wet suit or baggies, mostly well worn. He was the most beautiful man I had ever seen. The years following his first diagnosis changed

4

everything for us. Time no longer seemed to make sense. For the first year, I slept with my hand on his back or close to him, afraid of his death and losing him.

We had many good years after his diagnosis. We learned to appreciate life, each other, every day and every moment. We explored our spiritual beliefs and asked what we believed about death. I promise you he was on first name basis with a God that many people never get to meet as he spent every day in God's cathedral. He was shy but you would never know it, except for many of my friends who did not believe he even existed. Standing face to face with you, if you could manage to get him in that position, Pancho had a booming Southern drawl and could talk your ear off about the things he loved. He loved surfing, he loved Nova Scotia, he loved his children and was proud of both of them, and he loved me and let me know in a thousand small ways. Romance wasn't his strong suit, but I would have bouquets of wild flowers over the kitchen sink and every morning he brought me a cup of coffee in bed...a treat I will always miss.

Chapter Three
Squamous Cell Carcinoma/Unknown Primary

Pancho returned from the doctor's appointment late that morning. He was dressed in his now typical "doctor visit" attire, a golf shirt instead of his tee shirt and boat shoes, instead of his flip-flops. His face was solemn as he entered the kitchen. I had been waiting for him to return, holding my breath and pacing.

"What did the doctor say? What did you find out?" I asked, while standing at the door so anxious I could not wait for him to walk in. "Well," he grimaced, as he tilted his head to the left, "It's not good." He had been told the results of the biopsy done during surgery to remove the lymph gland that had hardened into a knot on his neck.

I held the paper he brought home in my hand. It was Stage 4 Squamous Cell Carcinoma, cancer, with an unknown primary.

"What does that mean?" I wanted to know.

"It means they can't find where it started. They do not know the primary source. But, it's already spread to my lymph glands."

We stood for a second frozen and stared at each other. He had found the hard knot on his neck in November and started with his primary care doctor. The diagnosis was confirmed with the surgery and biopsy in March. That moment we looked into each other's eyes knowing his life was terminal. The diagnosis brought our focus to the reality of death.

Something about our relationship changed after that lightning strike. There are moments and places in your life that you always remember. We were standing in our living room. The antique clock given to us by his Danish grandmother, Bedste, ticked quietly and rhythmically. I saw the look of fear in his eyes and listened to him apologetically share the truth he could no longer avoid.

He had really known since November when he had had the needle biopsy. At that time, he tried to make light of it.

"They said there are some 'thick' cells in the lymph gland." Pancho choked out the words. With the full reality on the table, we held each other and wept. At night, I would find myself staring at the ceiling, unable to sleep. With my hand on his back, I used magical thinking; perhaps I could somehow heal him if I kept it there all night.

Often warm tears of disbelief streamed down from the edges of my eyes to wet the pillow. Brigitte, a close friend, offered hope of healing with a spiritual book about spontaneous remission. We needed hope. We needed miracles. We needed magic. Spiritual books were a long shot. I had been on a spiritual path since the children were born but Pancho had little interest in things that could not be seen or touched.

I was living with the teachings of *A Course in Miracles*, which is a universal teaching, rather than a religion. It is a complete self-study spiritual thought system, one version of the universal curriculum of which there are many thousands. The goal of ACIM is happiness and peace. At that same time, I was providing hospice grief counseling. I had shared my spiritual insights with Pancho in the past though he never admitted he agreed with me. Now, with his cancer diagnosis, our spiritual life took on new meaning. Pancho became open to possibilities.

"You can read it to me," Pancho said and we began to take long drives so I could read it to him aloud. Virginia Aronson called the book "Celestial Healing". As crazy as it sounds it gave an account of a miraculous healing through the intervention of a hovering light. The author lived not far from us in Florida. This made it more personal. After being given a prognosis of only days to live and being told she would never leave the hospital, she begged an orderly to let her go home one more time to see her young son. The orderly agreed, but only if she promised to be back by morning.

The book described her experience. At home, while lying on her bed, her body froze, and she watched the room fill with a white fog. Her body seemed to levitate and through the window, she observed what appeared to be a disk shaped object 8 to 9 inches across. It scanned her body with a blue light...and she believes that day she was healed and lived to write the story of that healing blue light. Pancho listened.

Chapter Four
Miracles

We wanted to believe in miracles but the reality was we were both terrified. I continued searching for cures, for healing tools. Our reading expanded to all sorts of health and wellness books provided to us by Beth, my best friend since childhood. She brought her books in stacks. Of course, we tried everything. We flew to Mexico to have the mercury fillings removed from Pancho's teeth by a biological dentist trained by the expert, Hal Huggins, who wrote "The Root Canal Cover-Up."

Pancho's effected lymph gland was just below a root canal. Since neither the doctors nor the PET scans could find an originating source for the cancer, we hoped it might be in his mouth. We started raw juicing and put Pancho on an alkaline diet as a Nobel Prize winner had discovered cancer could not grow in an alkaline system. We poured through the books. I stayed up late at night researching his diagnosis on the Internet. I read a heap of medical papers I did not understand. I did understand his type of cancer was not good. Few people survived. I did not tell Pancho everything I read. I did not want to steal his hope.

We prayed for a healing. One night in March 2003, there was a full moon. While I lay in bed, it began shining through the blue glass gazing ball hanging in the window at the foot of our bed. The light shone like a beacon and it focused directly on Pancho covering him with a blue light. I turned my head to look at the time. It was 4:44.

For many years, I had been seeing Master Numbers (reoccurring digits such as 1111, 111, 222, 333, but especially 444). They appeared in phone numbers, license tags, a wide variety of places and I gave significance to the appearance of those numbers. I was not the only one. So had others, including Dr. Doreen Virtue who wrote "Healing with the Angels." She was a psychologist who had an angelic intervention that saved her life and changed her future and her work in the world forever.

Those numbers caught my attention and made me pause and think. I had developed my own personal meaning for those numbers as messengers. It was a language I had come to call the 'language of the angels'. I was in shock and began to tremble. The moon shining through the blue glass orb sending a blanket of light at 4:44? It had to be a miracle. The event stayed close to the top of my hopes for months. "What are the odds?" I asked myself. Each month I waited for another full moon, expecting it to make a second appearance. It never did. Each month it tracked a slightly different path across the sky. Never did I witness the light shine through the gazing ball on the full moon creating the same blue bath on his side of the bed.

For months afterwards, Pancho and I stood and watched the full moon rise over the ocean. I thought about the experience in March. Did it mean anything, except hope? Was it significant? I wanted it to happen again. I wanted it to shine through the blue globe to bring its healing light. It did not, but that night I dreamt about it happening.

In my dream, on the front of the blue globe there was a target marking the spot in the form of a cross. The upward arm was a feather. I awoke from the dream and looked at the clock, 4:44. I sat straight up and climbed out of bed. I wanted to see where the moon was in the sky. I stepped out onto the porch outside our bedroom and found it overhead.

The moon was 20 degrees south of where it had been the night of the blue light. I said my prayer asking for all the forces of God and the Universe to come into our being. The rest of the night, I was aware of an energy vibrating in the area of my heart. Our first blue light experience had been a miracle. Ultimately, living 10 years with stage four cancer and his diagnosis is practically unheard of medically. That and many other events over the next ten years gave us hope; the miracle of hope is of major importance for healing.

Healing requires faith and hope.

Chapter Five
Our Plan

I was in a unique position. I had been trained by my life experience. Women, men and their life stories and recovery from their grief had entered my life and I learned from my clients. I watched how others did their grief. I studied the process, and while I taught the normal reaction to them, I knew I could not say I truly understood what they were going through. I had not lost a husband.

I guess you could say all things fell in place for me to have the luxury of experiencing the roller coaster of grief unimpeded by the world. I anticipated the position I would be in financially and planned carefully. We learned Pancho had a form of terminal cancer when we were in our early 50s. Luckily, we had some life insurance. Not enough to enable me to be financially free but enough to know I could take 2 years to do the work of grief before I had to come to a serious decision about what I wanted to do in the future to supplement my income. I was always a careful money planner and had been working on a retirement plan with a financial advisor since we were in our early 30s.

We were lucky; we had stayed together, no divorce, built a foundation, a home and had the medical insurance in place for Pancho's illness. During the years he was ill; I often worked three jobs and saved everything I could. I had already learned if I wanted to travel, I needed to make it a part of my work. I started to take people on tours, do international talks and sell my books. In addition, the timing was right. I could retire from hospice with my insurance and a pension and draw social security. I had a cushion and a plan that allowed me to fully step into my grief and to enact the plan Pancho and I had put into place.

Pancho was very aware of my interest in After Death Communication (ADCs). When I first started experiencing them for myself, I would excitedly share. Over the years, I heard so many stories, true stories from people whose loved ones had died. As the deaths in our lives accumulated so did our experience. Before long Pancho was sharing his own stories, the signs and messages he received from his friends and family who had died: rainbows in the mist of a wave, an eagle landing on the ground before him. We talked often about the importance of him sending signs to me after he died.

When my sister Lissa was having a private conversation with Pancho near the end of his life, she bemoaned the idea of his leaving us. He responded reassuringly, pointing to a beetle on the floor,

"I'm not going very far. I will just be across the room. I may come as that bug over there."

If anyone was prepared with the admonition to SEND signs after they died, it was Pancho. He had been through too much with me not to come through with messages after his death if it was possible. Pancho knew I wanted, no, needed signs to get through his death and he agreed before he died to send them. I wanted extraordinary proof, undeniable proof for myself and for others.

Chapter Six
A Penny and Six Roses

The room was dark except for the glow of the fireplace and untimely Christmas tree lights. The sound of a jazz band wafted across the river from the neighbor's annual birthday party. Pancho breathed rhythmically. I sat beside his hospital bed thinking, no not thinking. I could not think because I was so caught up with what I knew was happening. Between songs, there was the sound of flapping baitfish and I could see the silver scales caught by the rays from the dock light. Maxine, our Weimaraner, lay on the floor at the foot of his bed, bewildered. We were counting down the moments of Pancho's life. Melissa, our daughter, took cold wash clothes from bowls of ice and hung them on her father's head like a misshapen hat.

He had gone from hot to cold, cold to hot. Most of the previous 24 hours he rarely slept until he was ready to let go and then he did. The end snuck up on us. Dale, his hospice nurse, had bathed him that day instead of letting the home health aide do the job. Pancho was alert and talking however when she came out to meet with Helen, the social worker, and me as we waited on the dock, she told us, "He's very weak, I think it's probably going to be tonight." With that, Dale gave me permission to leave behind the regiment of Seneca and all other medications except for those to manage pain. By that time, I was delirious with lack of sleep. I hovered over him.

During those last days, I was up with Pancho every couple of hours all through the night. I was beyond exhaustion and slept not far from him in the same bed his father had died in a year and a half before. In a trance, I did what I had to do to prepare. I called his family. Dean, his brother, came to spend the night. He stood by Pancho's bed and massaged his arms until he himself was so tired he fell asleep on the couch next to Pancho. Melissa went to sleep in the other bedroom.

At 10:00 o'clock, I gave Pancho 3 small drops of morphine in his cheek, as he could no longer swallow. I then dropped into a zombie-like sleep, only awakening at the time for his next dose of pain medication. My internal alarm clock woke me. Pancho was no longer breathing. He died a few hours after midnight at 2:22 AM. I knew the time. It was 2:15 AM when I woke. I did not realize he had been having long periods of apnea that night until his brother told me later. When I saw he was not breathing, I stopped breathing myself and with trembling hands, I called hospice.

For months we had been waiting for this moment. We knew it was coming. I did what I knew I had to do next, make the call. Then I came back and crawled into bed with him. When I put my head on his shoulder, he took four more breaths and then stopped breathing forever. I looked at the clock, 2:22. What followed was a blur. I remember waking his brother who was snoring on the couch and then Melissa. I remember lying in bed, in disbelief, with my head

15

buried on his chest. I sobbed and wondered if he was gone. Maybe he was not dead.

However, he was.

The hospice nurse came, a familiar face who worked after hour shifts, a woman I had worked with over my years with hospice. I helped dress him a final time. She left when she knew I would be okay and just as my sister-in- law, Cathy arrived. Cathy and Pancho's brother, Dean, sat with me while I cried. When the sun rose, I called the funeral home and waited. My sister, Beth, son Treve, and Page, his girlfriend, arrived. The house was full but Pancho was gone.

That afternoon, after his body was taken away, the women gathered on the dock in front of the house. It was a warm day, so warm the girls, Melissa and Page, took Pancho's paddleboard out on the river. The river was slowly rising with the incoming tide. Pancho and I sat on that dock and watched his father's body carried away from the same house on February 12, 2011.

Pancho and I had been blessed with so much time to talk during the 10 years since his diagnosis and when we did, we talked about our love, how lucky we'd been over our 39 years together, and how blessed we were in every way by our children and family. I told him when we wrote this book together after he died, he must help me from the other side. I said this in a very matter of fact way. He agreed. "What will your signs be?" I asked him. "Will you send a special bird? Which one?" I wanted to know. His father sent Eagles, which was one of his nicknames, his mother sent Pileated Woodpeckers, my grandmother sent

Blue Jays, my grandfather sent Crows, and my father had sent Red Cardinals.

"Will you send rainbows?" I asked. "I'll surprise you." he joked. That did not really satisfy me. I wanted specifics so I could be sure, but I accepted his answer. It must have been around 3:30 PM the day of Pancho's death and quite warm when the girls took his paddleboard out in the river to cool off. My sister Lissa, Beth and I watched from the dock. They all knew my belief in the continuation of life after death and the ability of our loved ones to send signs. I found myself looking up to the sky and asking, no not really asking, demanding in fact, aloud, "Okay Pancho!" I demanded, "You promised. I want signs!"

I had nervously been picking away at some rotting wood that once held an umbrella on the picnic table in times past. As I finished clearing the last bit of wood away, I found a penny that someone had placed there while building the table. While I was contemplating, "Could this be a sign?" I heard someone excitedly say, "Look, there are roses floating down the river!"

"Where?" I gasped. Melissa, who was at that moment sitting on Pancho's paddleboard, started moving to retrieve them. There were six long stemmed red rose buds, drifting south with the tide, and she successfully retrieved two. She paddled back to the dock and handed them up to me and we captured the moment with our phones.

We were all elated. Roses! Pancho knew roses floating down the river would be a special way to get the message across because in 2011 something similar had happened.

Chapter Seven
Egan's Roses

Egan, Pancho's father, died February 2011. That was not long after his wife, Joy, had passed, five months to the day in fact. At her memorial, Egan announced that he would not be long for this world. He was right. That was the first time we received roses on the river.

It happened after his memorial service a few days after Valentine's Day. I had saved some of the roses from Joy's memorial and dried them. When I was planning Egan's service, I thought it would be nice to use the dried flowers at the end of his ceremony. Like Pancho, Egan had been on hospice. He died peacefully in his bed. After his death, we were busy arranging for the service.

Egan had given me instructions. He wanted it to be a simple ceremony in his front yard by his grapefruit trees on the river. Egan asked a bagpiper to play taps. I was lucky enough to find someone not long before his death playing his pipes in the middle of a parking lot in front of the courthouse. I stopped to listen and asked for his card.

Preparing for Egan's service was difficult, as it always is, done in a trance of rapid movement, all consumed by that first stage of grief: SHOCK. In the confusion of activity, I wanted to make sure I had the money put aside for the minister and the piper. At the time, Pancho was still well, although his cancer had returned and he had begun a new round of radiation. He had done his best to keep that fact from his father. Pancho was lying on the couch in our living room while I prepared for Egan's memorial.

As I was trying to complete a checklist I said, "I'm going to find some thank you notes upstairs and put the money for the minister and the bagpiper in the envelopes. I think the best place to put them is on the kitchen table in your Dad's house so I'll remember where they are, but just in case I forget, will you please remind me?"

Pancho agreed. I climbed the stairs and reached inside the drawer where I keep cards. The drawer was characteristically stuffed with blank cards but it also held some other cards I had received from special people. I pulled out a handful, shuffled through them and found two blank thank you notes and envelopes. I hurried off leaving the drawer open.

Completing my task, I put the money in the cards, sealed the envelopes and left to go next door. As I entered Egan's house I noticed there was something different. While I had been away, Pancho's cousin had brought a bouquet of yellow Sunflowers. I paused to admire them.

I put the cards in place and then noticed a bright yellow envelope lying next to the Sunflowers with only the initials "P and S" written on the front. "Hum? Where did that come from? It must be from Sally," I thought lifting the card, and then I saw it had already been opened. I stood for a moment perplexed, not expecting what I had found. The card was not signed. Instead, there was a caricature of Egan with his prominent nose and one meant to be Joy. As an artist and an art teacher Joy was often creative. Apparently, in my rush, I had inadvertently picked up a card she had given me in the past. The 'P and S,' scrawled in her distinctive youthful round script, stood for Pancho and Shannon. Inside she expressed appreciation for all we had done.

What timing, I thought. It felt just as if Joy had sent a reassuring message of appreciation to emphasize they were now together and wanted to say thanks. That is exactly what she would have done in life. Writing thank you notes was something she was keen to teach the grandchildren, several times gifting them each a box of thank you notes with their other Christmas presents.

In addition, Egan apparently wanted to say thank you, too, with roses.

The crowd stood around the grapefruit tree and the piper played taps. Egan's service went well. I had planned to have a gathering on the dock to throw the dried roses from Joy's service ceremoniously into the river on the outgoing tide. However the guests left, and in the busyness of food and cleaning up, I had completely forgotten.

Michaela, a supportive friend, stayed behind to help clean up. I was standing at the kitchen sink washing dishes when I saw the dried flowers untouched and remembered. "Oh Michaela, I forgot to throw the dried roses in the river before everyone left. Let's go do it now."

It was late afternoon. We picked up the dried roses and walked onto the dock. The tide was moving out slowly that day from the south flowing toward the ocean. When I turned to look back down the river after spreading the dried roses on the water, I saw something floating toward us. The water was speckled with yellow roses coming in our direction. I ran quickly and got a net to scoop them up from the water. There were twelve yellow roses. Gathering them into a bouquet, I took them into the kitchen and filled a vase with water. They joined the yellow flowers Sally had brought and Joy's thank you card. I figured someone had thrown them into the river after Valentine's Day, but I did not care, they came to me.

Because of that experience, it felt RIGHT that Pancho would choose something similar a year and nine months later on the afternoon of the day he died to send as a sign. The red rose buds floated down the river only a matter of hours after Pancho's death. If we had not been on the dock at that exact time, had Melissa not been on his paddleboard, the swiftly moving tide would have taken them south with the current and we would have missed them. As it was, Melissa could only catch up to two. That day the current was moving fast and the roses floated in the middle of the river, not within reach.

Pancho's first sign was timed perfectly. We were all there to witness the flowers. We were even able to take a picture of Melissa paddling up to the dock with the roses in her teeth and then handing them to me. However, who would believe that Pancho would come through with two more signs of significance that day, including another thank you note in a card and a song.

I think people often have experiences of a special card showing up from the past at just the right moment and feel contact from their loved ones. It happened to me the first time in 1993 when a card with a very special message written in my Grandmother's handwriting fell out of a magazine on Mother's Day.

The second sign from Pancho that day was set into motion earlier in August of 2012. I was going to have my 60th birthday. The Steve Miller Band, who was popular when we first met in the early 1970s, was performing live at the Biltmore Estates in North

21

Carolina. Pancho was supposed to go with me but he backed out at the last minute because he was feeling worse than he was letting me know. "I just don't feel that great," he told me, "but you go with you sister and your friends. You know you'll have a good time."

I was disappointed and concerned, but Pancho had already bought the tickets and he wanted me to go. My sister Lissa, Beth, and Michaela agreed to join me for the short trip to North Carolina to hear the concert. The morning I left for North Carolina Pancho walked me to the car. He gave me a large envelope. When I opened the card inside, the words "I LOVE YOU," popped-up from inside the card. I smiled and took a selfie of the two of us with my phone. It was not yet dawn when he kissed me goodbye. Above us, we heard the owl call from the oak branch. I took the card with me to show my friends and placed it over the visor above the dash of his father's Cadillac.

We used Egan's Cadillac only occasionally, reserving it for road trips. We still called it his. It was in the garage across the street from our house. When Egan was on hospice, he had used the panic button on the car's clicker to call us if he needed help. He had a cell phone but could not see well enough to use it. The car horn was perfect and we could be next door in moments if we heard the loud blaring.

After Egan's death, I would hear a blaring horn rhythmically beeping and think of Egan. There was one time in particular when my colleagues were at the house dedicating an orange tree to Egan and Joy. We were planting it in their yard. I was in the midst of a ceremony in which I had been asked to describe traits I loved about Egan. In the distance, I heard the bleep, bleep, bleep of a blaring horn.

"That's Egan," I said with a smile.

On the day Pancho died, that afternoon, when the out-of-town company had left, I decided I would drive the short distance to vote. It was Election Day and I did not know what to do with myself. When I got into my Camry, the gas tank was completely empty. Melissa had been driving it. I was not surprised. It was only a mile so I took a chance and drove empty tank and all. I sat down in the driver's seat and looked over on the seat next to me. I saw a coin with a hole in the center. I picked it up to examine it. It was a Danish Kroner.

Melissa had come from Norway to be with her Dad and a coin must have inadvertently dropped out of her purse. She had recently made a trip to Denmark. Pancho's heritage was Danish. Egan was born in Denmark. He came to America when he was 8 years old. I held the coin in my hand and looked at it closely. Was it a sign from Pancho and Egan? I wondered. Later I placed it in a special box with the penny I had found on the picnic table and the rose buds from the river, which I had dried.

When I returned home from voting I could not find my cell phone. It was my new IPhone 5. The one Pancho had just given me for Christmas. He knew how much I loved my iPhone but had been impressed by one of my friend's later version with Siri. He figured that might ultimately save my life, as I was often texting when I should not. That habit drove him crazy. On our last drive to Nova Scotia in August, he told me to buy myself the phone as his Christmas gift to me. I had ordered it October and it was supposed to be delivered by mail. It never came. Finally, I wondered what had happened. When I called, I discovered it had been delivered to the wrong address and returned to Texas.

The phone company was very apologetic, and because it was a new model it was hard to find one in stock at the time, but they were able to find one not far from me in St. Augustine. When Melissa arrived from Norway and could take a turn caring for her Dad, I asked her if she would either stay with him or pick it up for me. She chose to stay with her Dad. He did not like me to leave for any length of time so I hurried off to St. Augustine. I had not been away from him for the last two months except for brief errands.

The world seemed strange. Everything seemed bright and had an unreal quality. I felt compelled to hurry so I could get back. As I was driving north over the Matanzas Bridge on A-1-A heading toward St. Augustine near one of Pancho's favorite surf breaks, a song came on the radio. It was Aerosmith, "I Don't Want to Miss a Thing." I listened to the lyrics. They expressed exactly what I was feeling at the time.

"I don't want to close my eyes, I don't want to fall asleep because I'll miss you and I don't want to miss a thing..."

I wanted to remember to tell Pancho about the song that expressed the way I felt. I reached for my phone, which I also used as a recording device and tried to record the song as it played on the radio. I was too slow and missed it, but instead I sang the chorus into the microphone so as not to forget and was able to share my thoughts with Pancho when I returned home.

The new iPhone was very special to me. It was his last gift, a well thought out gift of love from Pancho, so when I returned from voting and could not find it I was very distressed. I combed both houses. I had no success. I could not find my iPhone! I knew I was confused but I thought, "Could I have lost it already?"

A short time later Page found me. "Beth called my phone." She said, "She accidentally picked up your iPhone and has it with her." I used Page's phone to call

24

Beth. She and Lissa were only 25 miles up the road and they offered to bring it back. "No," I declared, "I'll meet you on I-95. If I start driving now I can meet you at the first exit north." I was in a hurry but when I sat in my car, I realized it had no gas. I decided to take Egan's Cadillac from the garage and headed toward the interstate.

It was late afternoon by that time. I turned west onto the bridge crossing the Intracoastal Waterway. The sun was blinding my eyes, literally. As I turned right onto the bridge, I had to squint and slowdown in order to see. I imagined the light which engulfed my field of vision to be similar to what I had read describing a Near Death Experience (NDE). NDE experiencers often report entering a tunnel filled with intense light.

I reached up and pulled down the visor in Egan's car to get the sun out of my eyes. When I did a card, fell down and hit me on the head. I looked at my name boldly written in Pancho's handwriting on the front of the envelope. I had placed the card there in August and had forgotten it. It was the birthday card Pancho's gave me on the way to the Biltmore in the early hours before driving to see the Steve Miller Band. I opened it to find the big pop-up "I love you" and an intimate message of appreciation. I could only smile at the events.

I continued driving north on I-95, and got off the exit to meet Lissa and Beth. They were waiting at the gas station. I pulled up beside them, jumped out of the car with the card in my hand and told them what had just happened. "Pancho sent me a card!" They exclaimed surprise and we all laughed together at the synchronicity of the roses and the cards.

It had been a very intense day and they had a long drive ahead so we set off in opposite directions on I-95, Beth and Lissa heading north to Jacksonville and me back to the Hammock. I pulled onto the interstate and turned on the radio.

There it was, the Aerosmith song: "I Don't Want to Miss a Thing."

I broke into tears as I listened again to the song I had heard going over the Matanzas bridge. It had been only two days since I had last recorded my own voice singing the chorus to that song. This time I turned up the radio and turned on my recorder. The recorder on my phone caught not only the song but also my sobs, sobs of appreciation and loss.

This was something I would never forget. It was at Matanzas Inlet, Hope Island, where we chose to celebrate Pancho's life one week later. All of what seemed carefully orchestrated signs, the roses on the river, signs from his Dad, and the thank you card from his mom, hearing Aerosmith on the day of his death just after the card fell down on my head seemed at the time overwhelming proof that Pancho was in fact sending me the signs I'd asked for. I appreciated the messages, but in actuality, they did not bring a lasting comfort. They were not enough, I wanted more, and he brought more.

On 11/ 11/2012 at a final paddle-out done in Pancho's honor, there was a very special sign witnessed by everyone present.

Chapter Eight
The Final Paddle-Out

After other friends and family members shared their stories and memories of Pancho, Sheryl, the hospice Chaplin, gave a beautiful message. Then the service moved to Pancho's favorite surf spot. It is one of the most beautiful stretches of beach in central Florida near Matanzas inlet 15 miles south of St. Augustine. The park is called Hope Island. It was also, the place I heard the Aerosmith song on November 4, just two days before Pancho died.

The afternoon had turned cloudy and windy and the ocean was rough. Over 20 of Pancho's friends participated in the paddle out. It took a lot of skill for the participants to paddle through the northeaster that was blowing. The group of men and women gathered in a circle, threw flowers in the center, held hands and lifted their arms in his honor. I watched from the shore along with many of the people who had attended the service.

Lingering until everyone had left the beach, I started walking up the long wooden ramp leading to the parking lot. I heard my cell phone chime. It was a text message from a friend. "It's 4:44 on 11/11, it said." I looked at my phone, it was November 11 (11/11) and it was 4:44 pm.

I turned around to look back at the ocean only to witness another miraculous event. A rainbow began spreading across the sky.

Just prior to that moment, the sky was full of dark clouds. I captured the picture on the screen of my IPhone, with the time, and date imprinted over the rainbow. By the time I reached the parking lot, everyone was admiring the rainbow and we watched together as it turned into a double. My phone started ringing with calls and pinging with texts from people who had already left the service, some of them driving north on A-1-A, and some of driving south. They too had seen it and were witnessing Pancho's sign. At moments like that, there are no disbelievers; it is hard to deny when so many share in a miracle.

I was thankful and reassured by the message. It helped me get through the next few weeks. I moved out of the first stage of grief: shock and denial, and slipped into the next stage, "anger," a stage of grief no amount of signs can comfort, not even the many rainbows that followed me almost everywhere.

Chapter Nine
Over the Falls

This was beyond anything I had ever experienced. Other losses in life, including grandparents, my father, my brother, and both my in-laws, were nothing compared to this. Surfers have a term for what happens when you are caught up in a wave and swept over with its breaking crest. It is called going "over the falls." Along with the wave's tons of water, you are helplessly swept up in a crest of confusing currents and slammed into whatever is ahead. The wave goes back to the ocean. You are left stranded, breathless and exhausted.

I had watched how others did their grief. I had studied the process. While I taught the normal reaction to them, I knew I could not say I truly understood what they were going through. I had not lost a husband. I was working as a hospice bereavement counselor the entire duration of Pancho's cancer but I had never experienced the death of a husband, a life partner of almost 40 years.

I had been supporting others through their grief as a counselor for the last 12 years of my career as a licensed mental health professional. I considered myself an expert on death. During those years, I sat across from hundreds of grieving people, listening to their sobs, their memories, their reflections, mirroring their expression of sorrow, encouraging them to keep moving or just to sit and be.

The amazing signs I received in the first weeks after Pancho's death did not bring relief from my grief. I had moved into the emotion found at the top of the list, anger. The anger phase of grief ground into me and I was mad! I was mad at everyone and everything. I just let myself be mad.

I would fuss at Pancho for not bringing enough signs, for leaving me with all of his business, boats, trailers, and a big house with a zillion oak leaves. Our house had been neglected for many years as we just coped with living. I knew it was not rational but I understood irrational anger is normal in grief, so I just allowed it.

For a brief time, Helen, a social worker/co-worker from hospice, supported me and for the long haul, I had my sister and Beth on a daily basis. They would spend literally hours on the phone listening to me sob and rage. I had many supportive people around and some unsupportive family members, but that was to be expected. I knew it was normal. I did not beat myself up for feeling it. I was not surprised, but it took many people around me off guard.

People expected me to be okay; after all, I had been so strong and positive during Pancho's illness. I looked good from the outside, functioning, even over-functioning, moving at a break neck pace trying to cram a lifetime into what we had left together. People assumed if Pancho had a clear PET scan that he was cured; he was in remission. I wish that had been so. I wish miracles would have happened, but I knew all about cancer.

Facing cancer at work and at home, I now knew death in both places as well. One of the hardest parts for me was my job with hospice during the years of Pancho's cancer. On more than one occasion, I sat in front of family members of patients who had died of the same cancer, Squamous Cell Carcinoma with an unknown primary.

In the beginning, I could barely make it through those sessions. It was excruciating. It took years to get past the agony experienced on the job, but as Pancho outlived his prognosis and showed clear PET scans, I adjusted to the reality that we only have today. I opted to live in the moment. I went into a conscious denial and attempted to squeeze every ounce out of life.

I worked full time for hospice and part time for other agencies, wrote two books, promoted them, traveled and did workshops internationally. The movement kept me numb enough to survive. My job with hospice was not an option; we needed the income and I was so very appreciative of the people who had built the hospital I worked for, developed the Oncology center, cared for my husband, paid my salary and provided Pancho's health insurance.

I put on a strong face and convinced myself and almost everyone around me I was okay. It was not until after Pancho's death that I allowed myself to grieve and then collapse into everything that I was really feeling.

31

Chapter Ten
Escape to Mexico

My family, friends, and amazing hospice co-workers continued to be supportive. Knowing I was facing Christmas and New Year's, Beth came to my rescue. I had always given clients the advice I had been taught in my hospice training. You can do three things at the holidays: you can do it as you have always done it, do something completely different, or skip it, knowing there is not ANY easy way.

All I wanted to do was skip it. I did not want to be around anyone or anything associated with Christmas. We had put up the special Christmas tree from Nova Scotia and decorated it in October. Together as a family, we had celebrated Christmas early as we looked at the tree lights and sunsets over the river.

I had been very interested in the Mayans, and the Mayan Calendar. During the years leading up to the December 21, 2012 date, I had done a number of workshops in an attempt to explain, simplify and reframe the fear so many people were experiencing as they heard the negative hype in the popular press about the end of the world.

For that reason, Beth came through with a lifesaving offer to help me cope with the holidays, which so closely followed Pancho's death. She offered to spend Christmas with me at Palenque, Chiapas, Mexico: one of the Mayan's most important cities in Central America. The site containing massive Mayan Pyramids and ruins is only partially excavated. It is one of the primary sites associated with the December 21, 2012 end date of the Mayan Calendar.

We had for years talked about where we wanted to be on that date. There could not have been a better salve for my grief. Pancho had made sure I knew he wanted me to continue to travel with Beth, so when she came up with this idea to cope with the holidays, I immediately agreed to the trip.

Chapter Eleven
Palenque and the End of the Mayan Calendar

The Mayan ruins of Palenque are located in the mist-shrouded jungles of eastern Mexico. No Christmas trees there. Our tree was left on the dock. Boats could enjoy the lights as they passed. Melissa was in Thailand, Treve was with Page's family, and the idea of not having to write cards, wrap packages, or listen to traditional Christmas songs was exactly what I needed. I avoided all stores, including the grocery store. Who needed to eat? I pretended it was not a holiday at all. No one in the world should be celebrating. Pancho was dead.

Beth planned our trip to Palenque. We flew into Cancun, spent the night and caught a Mexican airline to Chiapas, south of the Yucatan. An empty seat was between us on the airplane. Being seated next to an empty seat happened so many times after Pancho died.

In Chiapas, we rented a car and took a couple of "fieldtrips" before checking into our hotel. We visited several Mayan sites on our way to Palenque. Everyone waited for the "big" day, December 21, 2012, the day celebrating the end of the Mayan Calendar.

The next morning, I woke early to sit by the pool and watch birds. A single black bird came, by himself, followed by two large yellow birds, then hummingbirds and a tiny yellow bird. The birds flew close to me, catching insects in midair above the pool. "Is that you, Pancho?" I asked, stretching my imagination wanting everything to be a sign. However, I knew the difference. There was no question about a real sign and that day was going to be full of them.

I wanted everything to be a sign. I wanted to feel him close. Birds often act as signs. Nevertheless, I asked myself, "What does it matter?" Even if it is a sign, it is not enough. I had been fussing at Pancho. I wanted more comfort for my grief.

Beth joined me by the pool and we went on to breakfast. We had decided to stay another two nights in Palenque. December 21 had come and gone. The world had not ended. It had been a full day of rain. Hordes of people splashed and played in the mud creating a "Woodstock" type celebration.

At the Palenque pyramids, the young and old had gathered from all over the world. Most traveled to the site to commemorate the end of the calendar. Some wondered if it were the end of the world. I do not think anyone was convinced that it might not happen. Many held their breath. I felt like my world had ended. Pancho's certainly had.

Instead of celebrating, we drove to a small Mayan village outside of town. We brought with us an equinox prayer used many times at other sites and other equinoxes and solstices. In the village, we lit a candle and read the prayer together at 11:11, the purported official time for the "End".

35

A few local Mayans joined us. Even though we did not speak the same language, they seemed to appreciate our sense of ceremony. Perhaps 12/21 was not an "end" but a shift in energy, an invisible line crossed, the end of a Yuga cycle, of several celestial cycles. Perhaps now looking back, we can see how things have changed in our lives, but it did not appear that the world had materially changed. The 11:11 on 12/21/2012 had come and gone.

We spent the rest of the day looking out at the rain from our hotel room window. On December 22, the first day of the new calendar cycle, I stopped on the way to breakfast to pick up my umbrella. I had leaned it by the front desk the day before and had forgotten it. When I reached over to get it, Beth cried, "Watch out!"

I had not seen the green parrot perched right next to the umbrella. I had almost stuck my face in his beak. "Oh gosh," I exclaimed, "I didn't see him!" The next day while walking past through the lobby, I asked the hotel clerk, "Where's the parrot today? I almost knocked heads with him yesterday?" "Oh," the clerk said, "You mean Pancho." "What?" "Had I heard him correctly?" Chills ran all over my body. In those silent private conversations with my Pancho, I had asked him to give me THAT specific sign, his name.

"And, what a unique choice for a bird, Pancho." I thought in my inner conversation. A green Parrot named Pancho. I explained to the clerk in broken Spanish that my "esposo," husband, was named Pancho, and had recently died. It seemed another miraculous moment. I posted pictures of Pancho, the green parrot, on Facebook before leaving for Palenque to tour the site that day. As we pulled into the site's

36

parking area young boys, offering to guard the car for a small fee and sticking a package under our nose inundated us. I recognized the package. They were selling rain ponchos. There it was again, his name. At the ancient Mayan Pyramid site, we met Salvador, a handsome, pale-eyed local guide who offered to lead us. After some negotiations, we agreed. The first thing he stopped to show us on the tour was a ginger plant. Once again, I could not believe my ears.

The last week before Pancho died, Lissa, my sister, and I had taken him around the yard in the wheelchair and he had told us all about the plants but particularly the ginger plant. He made us go get a shovel and dig up the root and showed us how it could be used to make tea as well as act as a spice. Pancho had made a really big deal about the ginger plant, so when Salvador made his first stop on the tour entering the jungle at a ginger plant I was well aware of what it meant. Again amazed, I felt Pancho's presence.

Salvador turned out to be a well-educated guide with a very mystical history. He was born on June 21, the summer Solstice. His son was born 73 days later on Dec 21, the winter Equinox, and 73 days later was his next child's birthday on March 21, the spring Equinox, and two of his daughters were born on his birthday. The number 73 is a sacred number to the Mayans. It is the number of days separating the seasons marked by the Equinoxes and Solstices. Salvador was a special person.

He told us a meteor had fallen on the 21st near the waterfall in Palenque. He showed us a picture from his cell phone of a fireball someone else had taken at Palenque the previous day. Salvador became our

37

teacher and provided hours of history and information on the mystery of the Mayans and their calendar.

When we returned to our hotel after the tour, we met a Mayan Day Keeper. He and his family had just come from an event at Chichen Itza the previous day. His name was Dr. Jose Jaramillo. As we walked past him, his wife and children at the pool, he smiled and said, "Happy first day."

That stopped us in our tracks and we began our conversation. He had a DVD he had produced called, "The Alignment Within." It seemed like fate. We bought a copy of his DVD, went back to our room and watched it. He knew many speakers at the major sites for the Equinox celebration. We arranged for him to come to Florida.

What was even more astonishing was it turned out to be a full day of Pancho's. Pancho first came up with our friend the parrot, next the young boys who offered to watch our car selling 'ponchos' and again at the end of the day.

Beth and I were standing in the lobby trying to find an internet signal when a waiter walked by. "Pancho, Pancho, Pancho", he yelled across the lobby. My mouth fell open as I looked at Beth. Her eyes were wide. The Pancho he was calling was the same waiter who had been serving us all week. His name badge said Francisco. Pancho is the nickname associated with "Frank" in Mexico. I had not made the association.

The next morning, we tried to explain to Pancho, our waiter, that his name was the same name as my deceased husband. I said, "Mi Marido muerto". I pointed to heaven with, "su nombre Pancho." I pointed to his name badge. He lifted his eyebrows and said in a breathless stream the few words he had learned in English, "I love you, I love you, and I love you!" It was a bizarre thing to happen; but that is what signs are, bizarre, often out of place, and unexpected.

In his way, Pancho let me know of his love that morning. I needed that message as we prepared to leave. Facing home was an unwelcomed next step.

Chapter Twelve
Portaging

Part of the grief experience is a purging of things: possessions, pictures, papers, papers and more papers, Wills, Trusts, doctor bills, death certificates: mountains of pieces that require attention. Traveling tribes of American Indians used portaging each time they moved. They sorted through everything they owned to see if it should be taken with them.

Grief requires portaging of material things but more so emotional clutter, memories, and unresolved issues: things best left behind, things needing to be pulled out, examined, stored, or discarded.

After Pancho's death, during the process of purging, I found a string of letters, journals and writings I had done between his diagnosis, and his death. Many of these were tributaries we took along our ordeal with cancer to survive. Living against a deadline of death requires hope; hope for a cure, hope for a miracle, hope for emotional strength to endure. We had quite a few causes for hope over the years of his illness when you consider how long he lived past his "due date," the one given to him by the medical community. During the long years of cancer, there were many gifts of hope.

Chapter Thirteen
Back to Reality

When I returned home from Mexico, which had been an attempt to escape my grief at Christmas, the full impact of Pancho's death hit again. Each feeling and emotion arose and stood before me like a wall to climb. Often, all I could do was curl up at the bottom and wait for energy to deal with each eruption before I could move again.

My personal loss was triple fold. I had lost a relationship of almost 40 years. I retired from my position as bereavement counselor, a role that had provided a meaningful place and training ground for my own life. Those two losses occurred on the brink of my 60th birthday. I was passing into a new decade, one marking the last trimester of life and calling on me to contemplate my own aging and death. I was losing time.

Everything had changed. I had never once been without a significant male relationship. I had moved from home into a relationship and then met Pancho. We met and were together from then on. We just began and never took a step backwards. Not that we did not question or struggle through relationship issues together during our time. Ours was as much of a rollercoaster as any other relationship I have found over years of doing family counseling for others. We rode out our storms and only separated in anger for three days in all of that time.

I was back to daily uncontrollable bouts of crying. Max, (the Weimaraner) and I, now shared the king sized bed. Since Pancho's death, we both squeezed onto my half of the bed, neither one of us willing to sleep on "Pancho's side." Poor Max would roll her eyes and lay her head on my chest while I wailed. Max, as well as Lissa and Beth, who I called first thing every morning, patiently listened to me cry.

Often, I could not sleep and would walk around outside at night. I would look up at the stars through the dark branches of our massive oak trees, feeling small, completely alone, and lost. The family compound once held Pancho's parents across the street and our son, Treve, in the family cabin. Now our house was empty, too, except for Max, Miss Lily the cat, and me.

Melissa left for Cambodia not long after the memorial service. She needed a training course for teaching English as a second language. Melissa was, in truth, making her own grief escape. She continued from Cambodia to Thailand, then to Australia where she worked as a nanny. After seven months in Australia Melissa found comfort with friends in Norway. She again took a job as a nanny helping with two-year-old twins and a four-year-old. Her trek around the world was her own way of coping with the loss of her father.

Treve and Page were starting their new family, expecting their first son in April. Each of us had gone to our own corner. Each doing the best we could to make the journey through grief.

Chapter Fourteen
The Book Launch

There was one thing that helped me get through the last months of Pancho's illness. It was a book launch in France. During the summer of 2012, before Pancho died, I encountered a flow of spiritual synchronicities rivaling those that inspired my first book. These synchronicities returned our focus where it belonged, on the continuation of consciousness after death.

In March 2012, Melissa invited me to go to the UK with her and two friends. I accepted and booked the flight. We were to meet in London in July. She was to fly in from a six-week yoga teacher training in Rishikesh, India. We planned to meet at Heathrow airport. I had arranged travel for a few days to Cornwall in order to visit old friends.

I bought our tickets for the train before Melissa's arrival. After visiting Cornwall, we would meet her friends back at Heathrow, spend a couple of days in London, and then travel north, to Scotland where Melissa and her friends were staying.

Chapter Fifteen
Butch and the Cathars

In the meantime, I received an interesting letter from a man who had read *The Magdalene Awakening*. His story caught my attention. Robert Ellison, nicknamed Butch, was experiencing what is often described as a spiritual emergence, or a spiritual emergency. This was not uncommon in my world but foreign to his.

Butch was a Florida native, born and raised on the land. He worked with his hands. He was a hunter and an angler. He fearlessly waded through the swamps of the everglades with snakes and alligators. Butch was a contractor but also a professional musician with his own CD.

In a trance state Butch had been contacted by a woman from the past, a spirit, someone from the Middle Ages. Prior to the contact, his ears would begin to ring calling him to enter a deep meditation. Butch alone heard her voice. It echoed in his mind while she held him in a deep trance. This was completely beyond anything he had heard of or believed. He wrote to me describing the strange experiences and asked if I understood what was happening. I read his letters and listened to his story. The woman, who contacted him in spirit, was in Ireland, and told him she was born in the year 1212. She vividly recounted detailed events from her lifetime and a journey she had made from France fleeing pursuers in 1222. She also showed him her tragic end. She was murdered and thrown into the River Suir near the Rock of Cashel in Tipperary County, Ireland.

I recognized in Butch's story the history of the Cathars, heretics from southern France who were the target of the fourth Crusade by the Catholic Church. I was very familiar with the Cathars having become intimately involved in their history. I had traveled to France many times to the places they lived and died during the 30-year crusade that took place between 1208 and 1244.

Butch's story was similar to the one told by a psychiatrist in England named Arthur Guirdham who wrote a series of books, the first of which was one called *The Cathars and Reincarnation.* Arthur Guirdham uncovered an entire community of people who interacted with Cathar spirits, not unlike the one Butch called Cedi.

The Cathar ceremony, called the Consolementum was performed for Pancho just prior to his death and I read it at Pancho's memorial service. I want it done for me when it is my time...it is very simple and goes like this...

First, a double kiss of peace on both cheeks...Then, the words: "You have completed your divine service well, and will now return to the realm of angels. The Holy Spirit fills your physical body as it prepares to return your soul to the great Oneness of the Divine where we will all dwell together again. May you make a good end. May you release your physical body with gentleness and grace as you return to pure spirit. We are separated from heaven by only the thinnest veil in our physical lives, and you prepare now to cross through that veil and into the light of pure love and the divine arms, which await you. The embrace of our Mother-Father God calls you home where we will all be together soon in sweet reunion."

It was not a coincidence Butch found my book. I could explain much of what he was experiencing, but unfortunately, at the same time this was happening, my own personal life drama was beginning to play out.

Chapter Sixteen
Metastasis

Sometime in mid-2012, Pancho's cancer had shown up again, this time in his lungs. It was serious. It was a fast growing cancer, small cell carcinoma. The doctors removed half of his lung and started a round of chemotherapy and radiation. The prognosis was not good. Pancho privately began to make a decision about his future, not really sharing the details of his condition with anyone.

He loved Nova Scotia. We had been traveling there together since we were in our early twenties, to a home that had belonged to my grandparents. We returned repeatedly with our children. In the years leading up to Pancho's death he discovered some amazing, private surf breaks, over 40. These he claimed as his own. Pancho spent time exploring coves and beaches, surfing, doing the things that he loved to do, in the heaven he knew, Mother Nature.

In the spring of 2012, he made the decision to take a trip to Nova Scotia with Max our dog that had belonged to his parents. I knew he had things to work out that only he could do within himself. I continued making myself more and more busy to cope with what I really did not want to know. I stayed in Palm Coast to work my hospice job.

In July, Pancho came back from Nova Scotia. Soon after his return, I left to meet Melissa for our trip abroad. Because of Butch's story, I planned a side trip to Ireland to explore places he vividly described. Then, an amazing synchronicity occurred. It was something that was helpful for both Pancho and me. It was something that kept our focus on the bigger reality of who Pancho really was, not merely a dying body, but an eternal being.

Mary Duncan, the woman who joined us as we prayed the Consolementum for Pancho, was a friend I had known for many years. She was a fellow Cathar lover. We had connected some time ago at the White Eagle Lodge. She now lived outside of London and was currently working at the London Lodge near Kensington High Street.

Grace Cook, an amazing medium who brought comfort to many during the World Wars, founded the White Eagle Lodge. Grace Cook and Mary Duncan had been a part of my story in *The Magdalene Awakening*. In 2001, Mary and I had traveled to Iona, Scotland together. I wrote Mary, and told her I would be in London a brief time in July. I also told her a little about the unfolding new "Cathar story" and possible link to Ireland.

She wrote back that Colum Haywood, Grace Cook's grandson and the publisher for the White Eagle Lodge had recently facilitated a workshop on the Cathars. She said Colum would be interested in meeting with me if he was in London while I was there. The date I would be in London was Friday, July 13, 2012 and Colum was available. We met at the lodge and during our conversation; he asked if I would like to be a contributor to a book, he was publishing through

Polair Publishing. The book was a compendium about the Cathars.

I was extremely pleased at the invitation, not knowing what my contribution would be at the time but I immediately accepted. That was July, the book was to be published in October, and Pancho died that November. The speed of events was unfathomable but the process of writing the chapter for "The Cathar View" was healing and inspirational for both Pancho and me.

My chapter contribution actually took form starting immediately as Butch's story began to unfold. The information Butch had been receiving from his medieval friend expanded upon Cathar history, and the true message of the Cathars. As I was writing, I read the chapter aloud numerous times to Pancho and during the last weeks of his life; it was a reminder of hope, hope for life and a relationship that continues beyond death.

During the time he spent in Nova Scotia alone, he was making peace with his life and death. His plan was well thought out. Having had cancer for almost 10 years he knew exactly what he wanted.

Chapter Seventeen
Pancho's Last Surf Trip

In August 2012, when I returned from Europe, we immediately attended a family reunion. I noticed, for the first time, a Band-Aid covering a small knot near Pancho's incision from his lung surgery. We all noticed he was not feeling himself. After the reunion, Pancho let me in on his plan. He told me he had to go in for another biopsy and wanted to leave immediately after that surgery to go back to Nova Scotia. He said he wanted to take Treve with us so they could surf together.

We would drive up the coast and Treve would fly up later. Pancho even purchased a new wetsuit so I did not realize how serious his condition was. He asked me to take my personal leave from hospice and he asked me to sit down and listen, "I want you to do exactly what I ask, no arguments. You need to slow down and just be with me. I'm being selfish now but you have to promise."

His amazing oncologist, Dr. Richard Weiss, who had supported him in such a personal caring manner, scheduled the biopsy to remove the lump the following week, and had him released from the hospital to leave for Nova Scotia within another week. I wanted to be as upbeat and positive as possible, always avoiding the obvious outcome with denial. I was coping in that manner. I continued to hope for a miracle and believed a miracle could happen. There are many kinds of miracles; there are many kinds of healings. I cleared my leave with my supervisor at hospice and we began our drive together to Nova Scotia for the last time.

Chapter Eighteen
Nova Scotia and John of God

We headed north at the very end of August 2012. Pancho's doctor had prescribed enough pain medication so he could be comfortable. In a strange way, it felt like we were 20 again. Pancho was in good spirits and hopeful. He told me that when we returned he would consider doing further treatment if the doctor felt it would help.

The biopsy showed the lump was the original cancer, squamous cell carcinoma, and they had no idea how far it had spread to other parts of his body. We talked honestly about our lives, our feelings, death and the future. I, who had written so often about life after death, kept upbeat. Together we talked about doing this book," together" meaning with his help from the "other side." He, above all else did not want me to get emotional or cry. I complied.

Instead, Pancho planned a surprise. We had traveled together to the Knights Templar sites in America on other trips. I had been doing research for years working on a book about the Knights Templar. We had also found a person from history who connected to the Knights Templar, Prince Henry Sinclair, and a voyage that had purportedly been made in 1398. Prince Henry had arrived at the northeast corner of Nova Scotia in a place call Guysborough.

Pancho said we could drive to the monument commemorating Prince Henry's arrival and take the coastal road down to Shelburne. The prospect of putting our feet on the same beach as Prince Henry gave me great joy. We both felt guided on this trip. With some unexpected luck, we were given directions to what was thought to be the actual site where Prince Henry came ashore. As we stood at the spot, feet in the wet sand, an eagle circled over our heads. An eagle had flown above us when we crossed the border coming into Canada and had landed on our lawn the day Egan died. Like rainbows, eagles followed us everywhere.

We drove on to Jordan Falls stopping at the Gold River and Oak Island tied to Prince Henry and his history in Nova Scotia. It is in Shelburne County, Nova Scotia. The house built in the 1700's still stands. It has belonged to a long line of family members. My brother owns the house now. Prior to him, my aunt, the daughter of our grandfather, Leslie Brydan McKay, Sr. owned the house.

The house has always been a part of my life. It was the same for my siblings, a very special place since childhood. It had been a part of Pancho's life since he was 22. We drove there our first spring together in 1974 and many more times over the years. Nova Scotia represented somewhere unchanged across our lives, the same house, the same furniture, the same apple trees and brook.

For us, it was 'up there' in the same way heaven is 'up there,' to most people. We spent our first days in Nova Scotia taking drives to Pancho's favorite beaches and walking barefoot in the sand. He showed me some of his surf breaks and we settled into the little house that had been so special to both of us.

Pancho slept in my grandmother's bed. It was more comfortable for him to sleep alone in the old bed that sagged in the middle. He was in some pain. I camped out in the living room where I slept on a mattress on the floor. I tried my best to slow down and even write. Pancho had hoped if I was there with him, that I could use my time to write the book about the Templar Knights.

I did spend time finalizing the chapter for *The Cathar View,* and we talked about how amazing it was that all had come to fruition so quickly. I also planned my trip to the south of France in May for the book launch, hoping that Pancho would still be alive. Pancho told me he was proud of my writing and wanted me to continue.

We took our last walk together to the railroad bridge. It was only a short distance from Mammy's house. From the trestle, which had been converted into part of a walking loop through Jordan Falls, Pancho took his last picture. It was of the full moon. It was the first of three full moons we had together in Nova Scotia that trip. It was the same moon he had introduced me to in our early 20's. The moon we would watch rise over the ocean. I took a picture of him taking that picture. I hung behind as we approached the top of hill on which the house stood. I took a picture of Pancho's last walk home.

The day after our walk, he fell while getting out of bed and never walked for more than a few steps again without my arms around him. As he felt his health deteriorating, he made the decision to spend the last days before his death in Nova Scotia. We lived in the moment and took one day at a time. I wanted more than anything to honor his wishes.

There were moments of hope, moments of believing in the possibility of a miracle. For years, I had heard of and read about John of God. Most recently, he had come up in numerous ways for me. John of God is a healer in Abadiania, Brazil. He has been healing people for the last 35 years. Before his death, Wayne Dyer talked about the "long distance healing" John of God offered. I did some research, and discovered a picture could be presented to him for the purposed of healing. If he put an X on the picture, you were directed to come to Brazil to be healed. Since Pancho was too sick to travel, we asked for the long distance healing.

We photographed Pancho, as directed, all white from all four sides, and found a representative in Brazil. We were directed to pray and meditate and at 1:00, Pancho's picture would be presented. My sister Lissa, in Florida, and good friend Sally, in Nova Scotia, joined me in meditation.

We were given hope when something very synchronistic happened. After an hour with lit candles and prayers, I went online. I was surprised to see a message, which said

"Subject: Hello from the Casa at John of God in Brazil." To my astonishment, it was not from the person we had asked to take Pancho's picture before John of God but from a friend, Carol Pessin, who was in Brazil.

From: cpessin
Subject: Hello from the Casa at John of God in Brazil

Date: Thu, 6 Sep 2012 13:02:23 –0400
Hello!

All is well here at the Casa De Dom Ignacio. Very peaceful, full of interesting people, from around the world, all coming to heal. John of God works at the Casa. A healing place that welcomes everyone at no charge. He sees people Wednesday thru Friday. Last week I had a spiritual surgery. There is a 24-hour rest period after each spiritual surgery. You are asked to stay in your room and sleep. John of God also performs physical surgeries when requested, but only on people 18-52 years of age. The healing by the entities comes through faith, prayer, and asking to be healed. The entities already know what we need to heal. But it is important here to ask, and have faith that we will be healed. There are several entities that are here to heal people, including Dom Ignacio, founder of the Jesuits, St. Francis Xavier who was one of the first Jesuits, Dr. Valdivino who has been working on me. Also St. Francis, John the Baptist, and King Solomon appear here. A new entity appeared here last year. When asked its name, it said call me 'Love.' This entity would not give its name. When asked why, 'Love' said that if the name was given, the Casa and surrounding village could not hold all of the people that would want to come! The entities also come through at night to do surgeries while we sleep...If you would like me to place any names in the healing prayer basket, I need the name, birthday, where they live, and what is to be healed. I will write it on a white paper and put it in the Healing Prayer Basket at the Casa. This is very powerful healing. They say that many people have been healed this way.

Blessings, Carol

I immediately wrote back:

Dear Carol,

Carol, I am still in shock. I received your email immediately after Pancho's picture was taken before John of God...At first I thought it was from Adrienne, the woman who was representing him. When I realized it was you and you were there, I was shocked. It was such an affirmation when your email arrived in such a timely manner. Last night after we sent the request for the herbs, my husband said, "I tasted 'Brazilian Wood." Your email was a blessing and a sign. Thanks so much.

With love and appreciation, Shannon

Carol agreed to take Pancho's picture before John of God once again and to get any herbs he recommended and send them to us. It seemed almost unbelievable, the timing of her email arriving and that night Pancho tasting "Brazilian Wood." He could not explain what or how he knew it was Brazilian Wood, but it was real to him. Was it a sign from John of God? Once again, we were hoping for a miracle.

I wrote to tell the story to my friends and family:

Dear All,

In the spring, the healer John of God was everywhere it seemed, literally. One day I Googled something and the 'John of God' webpage just appeared. We all had talked about visiting the Casa in Brazil for Pancho and in truth out of shear curiosity but as I said, his name kept coming up and I told Pancho we should go.

I found a guide and a trip leaving in May but Pancho said, "No. The only way I'd go is if I got sick again." "But," I pleaded, "Why not do it BEFORE? Please let's go!" Pancho went to Nova Scotia instead...

I requested a long distance healing. Miraculously, a friend, Carol Pessin, was in Brazil and emailed me at exactly the time Pancho's picture was taken before John of God. Carol is a healer and a Lightworker who I met at the Magdalene Gathering in Connecticut in 2007. I had seen her at several Lightworker conferences but she did not know Pancho was so sick. That synchronicity seems a miracle and we are hoping for one.

With Love, Shannon

Once again, we were all hopeful (especially Lissa), hopeful, but realistic too. John of God did not put an X on Pancho's picture to tell him to come to Brazil. He only prescribed herbs, which Carol later sent. The reality was that after a few days of improvement and hope, Pancho continued to get worse and I remembered only God knows "the Big Picture."

Chapter Nineteen
Continuing Sunrises

Elizabeth Palin, the psychic medium, once told me about the first time she met her teacher, Miriam. This was when Elizabeth and I were recording our conversations for *Finding Elizabeth*, a book I was writing about her life and work as a medium. Her teacher was speaking before a group in England about healing and during the talk, she mentioned that her husband had cancer and was close to death. After the talk Elizabeth approached her, "If you are a healer," she asked, "Why don't you heal your husband?" Miriam smiled, "Healing happens in many ways, my dear, sometimes the healing is death."

We hoped for healing, but I was well aware that life is terminal and no matter what, one of us was going to die first. I realized it would most likely be Pancho. Our days continued, one sunrise to the next. From the mattress on the floor in the livingroom, I watched Netflix to distract me and every morning I would gently push the door open to see if Pancho was awake.

"Am I dead?" he'd say in a raspy voice, or "I'm not dead yet." Pancho's dark humor. I always told him he should have been a comedian.

In truth, there was always a knot in my stomach as I stood outside that door. I tried my very best to honor

Pancho's wishes during the last months of his life. We had a routine. While in Nova Scotia, it would be my gently pushing on the door to his room, it would get stuck on the undulating floors of the old house. I would go lie on the bed, massage his feet or listen to his dreams, or just be silently with him.

When he was ready, we would move to the living room with his arms wrapped around me for balance. I helped him sit up on the couch. He spent his day soaking in the birds outside the window, the sounds of their call, the skies, and the trees. He often would say, "Everything is so beautiful."

I washed his hair and bathed him. I shaved him. It was the first time I had ever shaved a man's face. Then I would do my best to just listen, not talk too much which I had a habit of doing when I was avoiding emotion. There were no tears allowed and we talked about how lucky we had been in our life together.

When Pancho made the decision that he did not want to go home, the family had to be contacted. Pancho wanted to tell them himself. Those conversations were so hard for him. He procrastinated as long as he could but finally began with his brother Dean and then our daughter Melissa. Melissa was in Norway. She did not want to believe he was as sick as he was.

I was in the room when Pancho told her, "This is selfish Melissa, but I would like you to come if you can." When Melissa realized he was truly failing, she booked the first flight. His brother Dean and his wife Cathy flew up as well. Treve and Page had arrived shortly before and brought with them the surprise that there would be a new Andersen entering our world. It was a great joy for us to learn that our first grandchild was on the way. With a grandchild on the horizon, Pancho considered fighting to live. However, the reality was, he could not hold down food.

The family arrived and gathered around. We decided to have an last Thanksgiving meal long before Thanksgiving. Cathy cooked her first turkey. Melissa peeled potatoes and we made apple pie. The kids picked fresh apples from trees in the front yard. Our happy noises drifted into Pancho's bedroom which was just off the kitchen. He told me he loved hearing us all prepare the meal.

We gathered in the house that Dean and Cathy rented on the Jordan River to eat. There was much love and laughter and many pictures documenting that day. The rental house was more suited for Pancho's care. After Page, Melissa, Dean and Cathy left for home, Pancho, Treve and I remained behind in their rental house.

I sent a newsletter home for family and friends via email.

Dear All,

Last night Treve took Melissa to the airport. They left about 2:00 PM and she flew out about 10:00 PM. Pancho is now having a hard time swallowing even his dissolved medications. He was not able to enjoy the feasts we prepared together. We made a list of pros and cons about staying or going home, the weather and comfort being a real determiner for us. Pancho also wants to see the fall leaves one more time. I finally talked him into going to the emergency room to get assistance for his abdominal discomfort, but the doctor just told us he had a blockage and if she were to treat his condition, it would mean admitting him for surgery.

We both adamantly declined. No more hospitals! I had promised Pancho. His quality of life is everything now and though he is weak and tired and only walks while being supported, he is peaceful and for the most part comfortable. He has a hard time breathing, but when he takes the medication, it helps.

We really enjoyed having both Treve and Melissa here. I have not heard so much laughter in forever. They cut up as if they were 8 and 10, playing pranks, hitting and teasing each other. It was nice to have the laughter. Melissa spent the hour before she left in a private conversation with her Papa and Pancho was very satisfied and happy by whatever they discussed. The first thing he said in the wee hours of the morning was, "Where do you think your daughter is now?" We decided she would still be flying. She had to get back to Norway where she is starting a new life. The family she lives with loves and supports her. Pancho and I both agree we have no fear for Melissa. She will survive and thrive at whatever she ends up doing. We are proud of both our children. Treve is supportive. He has been sweet and cooperative, and I am so grateful he is here.

Dean and Cathy are leaving early today, so we will have access to the house they rented until October 5th. It's much more comfortable, decorated nicely, and everything is new but both Pancho and I have been very content to be in Mammy's home, in Mammy's bed with a WW II Navy blanket to sleep under. Pancho spends his days on the antique "fainting" couch in the living room. From there he can watch the sunrise from the window as he is doing right now. We have seen most sunrises and two full moons since we have been here.

Pancho continues to think I am Superwoman. He sends me to take care of all the details. He is very happy to have my full time and attention, from washing his hair to scratching his head on command. It took me almost two weeks to slow down enough to understand what he wanted, and I am learning many lessons.

I have listened to things he is experiencing at night where he accumulates knowledge about life and death and acquires understandings beyond his ability to express in words. "I love you," falls from his lips multiple times during the day and night. He is so appreciative that I am able to do this for him.

He has gone from being hot to cold, desiring cold to warm drinks, from opening all the windows to cuddling under blankets even when it is in the 70s outside. The weather could not have been more beautiful and the family around us could not have been more supportive. We have watched a thousand movies. On sleepless nights we watched the entire Mad Men series. That is very bizarre, as I never watch TV at home. I thought I would be able to accomplish so much writing while here but just cannot focus.

I do not think Pancho would change a minute of our time here. The whole family looked at the pictures I scanned on my computer of the kids growing up. Everyone laughed. Melissa posted many of them on Facebook. Considering this is the epilogue to Pancho's life, all is going very well.

We are now planning to load up the camper and truck, put a bed in the back, and drive home. Pancho's wish initially was to die in Nova Scotia. Now he realizes there are drawbacks; death just does not always come so easily and does not always happen when you are ready.

Home is sounding better, with a hospital bed at Egan and Joy's house. There, he can look out over his own river. He had the opportunity to say good-bye to Nova Scotia, which was his last desire, and Treve has ridden the waves for him, which brought him great joy. The most joyous thing was having the family together, especially just the four of us. Our dream was to retire to Nova Scotia when we were old. I told Pancho, "Some people consider 61 old. So in a way we lived our dream, if only a short while."

Love, Shannon

The decision was made. Home was increasinly more inviting as the days went by.

Chapter Twenty
Our Christmas Tree, The Westford Knight Stone and Lowell, Massachusetts

We talked most often in the predawn hours of the morning. At sunrise, Pancho would position himself to look out over the Jordon River. The trees along the bank were full of bright apples. Through those apple trees, Pancho watched the sun come up each day. Pancho lay on the sofa. I sat next to him in an old overstuffed chair, the one with paws on the end of its arms. It was in that chair I had sat, on Papa's lap, when I was five.

Pancho lay on the same couch I had sat on with boyfriends when I was fourteen. Letting go of his wish to die in Nova Scotia was difficult for Pancho. He was such a private man and he wanted a private death but he finally decided to go home one last time. Winter was approaching; the house was not set up to keep us warm. He was too weak to fly and even driving was going to be incredibly trying.

Treve and I prepared for the trip. I was relieved to learn the hospice team I had worked with for 12 years would prepare our house before our arrival and help keep Pancho peaceful and as free of pain as possible. I was thankful I would not have to do it alone. There was one thing I promised Pancho, "You don't have to die in pain. You can have a peaceful death and my co-workers at hospice are the experts at palliative care."

Pancho's wish to see the fall leaves was certainly granted. The trees were in full color the day we chose to leave. For two years, he had carefully pruned a blue spruce at the edge of the woods. Pancho wanted to bring it home for Christmas. The last task Treve and I had to accomplish was to cut down the Christmas tree. We worked under Pancho's supervision. He gave us directions from the couch through the screened window.

Both Treve and I worked silently, following his orders, cleaning, packing, and closing down the camper, loading the surfboards on their rack and strapping the Christmas tree down on top. In the back of the SUV, we made a bed. Treve drove and I navigated. Pancho, lying in the back looked out the window for his last drive down Jordan Bay road. He gazed out the window at the fall leaves and the river.

We left early in the morning. It was a long drive to get to the border. We wanted to make it there on our first day. The GPS said it was 5 hours and 18 minutes from Shelburne Nova Scotia to Calais, Maine, 222 miles. Pancho was so uncomfortable he did not want to drive more than 6 hours but we also wanted to make the trip as quickly as possible.

At the border, we experienced a sort of astounding event. While sitting in line to take our turn with the border guard, the man in the car next to us said, "They aren't going to let you take that tree over the border." "What?" I exclaimed, "My grandfather used to bring us a tree every year." "No" the man said, "They stopped that years ago."

We all moaned, especially Pancho. He had chosen this tree so carefully. We started praying, me out loud. It did not look good. The border guard, wearing Gestapo looking, knee high leather boots, was examining the car in front of us as if the driver was a terrorist. He opened the back, looked in all sides, walked around the car several times and took an extremely long time before releasing the car owner.

It was our turn. With trepidation, we pulled forward. The border guard leaned in the front window and asked, "Where are you from?" "Florida" we all three piped in, Treve handing him our passports. He then looked in the back seat, "What's going on back here?" he asked, as he saw Pancho lying in the back. "He's a hospice patient", I told him, and "We are taking him home." His expression changed as he grasped our situation. "What's this," he squinted in the direction of the tree, "A Christmas tree?"

"Yes," I replied weakly.

The guard paused. We held our breath. Pancho tried to look even more pitiful than he already did. "I'm going to walk back here and get your tag number," he said." He walked around the back of the truck and camper with a pad in his hand. When he returned he handed us our passports and waved us on.

A cheer went up in the car as we departed! We were so relieved! "Thank you Archangel Michael," I exclaimed as I had called on him outloud while sitting in line.

We continued south and stopped at the first motel past the border. Having been in Nova Scotia for a number of months, no one had any American money, not even change. Ahead we faced numerous tolls on the Maine Turnpike. I was so confused and upset; I could not remember my pin numbers for my debit card. That meant we were in a pinch. After trying three times I was locked out and having no cash was upsetting Pancho.

After spending the night, we set out again. Finding cash was our priority. On the phone with my bank, I attempted to get a new pin. I was transferred from one supervisor to another. I was getting very frustrated and angry. Luckily, the tollgates were accepting Canadian quarters so we kept moving south. I set the GPS to a town that I knew would take us around the big city traffic. Pancho wanted to avoid any congestion. I typed Westford, Massachusetts into the GPS. While Treve drove, I continued asking for someone else to help us unlock our debit card. Near the end of one phone call, I heard Treve ask, "Mom, where do I go?"

The GPS had ended its destination. I looked up just in time to see we were right next to the Westford Knight Stone, one of the places Pancho and I had visited on our tour of Knights Templar sites on the East Coast. "Stop!" I said, "Pull into the school. I know where we are!" We pulled over. I was jolted and intrigued by the synchronicity. Treve and Pancho were less so. All Pancho wanted was cash! I talked Treve into walking back to take a picture of the Westford Knight Stone, while I stayed on the phone asking for yet another supervisor.

The stone blended in with the sidewalk in the small Massachusette's town. It was not a well-marked site. On the slab was a carving of a knight with a broken sword, indicating a fallen comrade. The armor was from the Gunn clan, cousins to the Sinclairs. This pre-Columbian marker was one of the "proofs" that Prince Henry Sinclair had in fact traveled in

America. Westford is a town; the monument is in a neighborhood; that the GPS should end at that spot was unintentional.

Back on the phone, I finally got someone to understand and I was given a new pin number. We drove to the closest ATM. To my amazement, the town right next to Westford was Lowell, Massachusetts. Pancho's mother had been born in Lowell. I had always thought Joy, Pancho's mother was born in Cincinnati, but Dean had mentioned a few days before that she was born in Lowell. So, it was in Lowell I was able to get "plenty of cash" to Pancho's great relief.

We traveled home through a spectacular display of foliage but the trip was somber and few words were spoken. Treve's eye contact with me was sufficient. Our fear was, or at least my fear was, that Pancho would not make it all the way. He was really having a hard time traveling.

We finally arrived home. A hospital bed was waiting in his parent's house, which remained uninhabited and furnished with the familiar family things. There were no steps to climb. It had a handicapped bathroom. The bed was placed so Pancho could look out over the river, watch the sunset and see deer grazing in the neighbor's yard.

From watching sunrises, we went to watching sunsets. Within a couple of days, the Christmas tree was up. My sister helped me decorate it. Pancho spotted a rainbow painting the sky directly over the river and brought my attention to it. The river was full of schools of small fish, more than any of us had ever seen before. The fish continued to fill the water with undulating waves for many days. We moved into the last chapter of Pancho's life, supported by hospice.

Chapter Twenty-One:
Don't Postpone Your Joy

During the last two years of Pancho's life, I worked three, twelve-hour shifts for hospice. In addition, I had two other employment contracts and my own business, Sacred Escapes Publishing which required publishing books, promoting books, conducting workshops, and taking people on personal tours of sacred sites.

I kept so busy I could not think. I did not want to think. I knew...

Travel was my distraction and joy during those years. Beth, Lissa, and I, and sometimes Pancho, would take short weekend trips. As I look back now, I think the intense activity was an attempt to cram an entire lifetime and 'old age' into our remaining time together.

Pancho and I were so different. He was laid back, private, and loved time by himself and being in nature as much as anything. I was a Leo; he was a Cancer. I liked going out, he loved to be at home, his home. He loved waking early and spending a couple of hours in the morning reading the paper, doing his exercises, running or riding his bike and then surfing and fishing. He made the decision when we moved out of the chaos of Jacksonville to the small Hammock, that he would fish and surf at least for a short time every day.

Because he worked for himself on his Mariculture farm-growing clams, he could do that. Eliminating stress is an important measure to use when fighting cancer, as important as nutrition and exercise. He slowed his life down and did his best to enjoy his days. He napped in the afternoons and slept with the cycles of the sun. Pancho was usually in bed just after dark and rising before daylight to have his quiet time.

On one of our short weekend trips to North Carolina, Lissa, Pancho, and I stayed at the Biltmore Estates. We stopped to eat at a restaurant that served fresh organic vegetables. We took tons of pictures creating good memories. I still carry the pictures with me on my phone. It was on that trip that we found our motto "Don't Postpone Your Joy."

In the parking lot, we saw that phrase printed on a bumper sticker. It became our chant. I had always imagined living a long life with Pancho, being old, and walking on the beach together in our retirement years. When he sat me down in August to tell me to take my personal leave, that we were going to Nova Scotia, I was so caught up in the buzz of my life, the never ending cycle of activity that kept me in denial and provided health insurance for his treatment, I did not fully comprehend what was going on. I just did not want to know. I preferred to stay numb and pretend or hope for a miracle.

So did Melissa. On the outside, I said I was in denial. Nevertheless, in reality, I, if anyone, knew the ravages of cancer after working for hospice so many years. Cancer and death were real for me. I had been innoculated by my job, you could say, by my day-today work. Counseling the grieving had required taking on an armor to protect myself. I mastered an ability to dull my emotions and feelings in order to cope.

Following Pancho's death, I had done the raging. I was so angry at everything and everybody. I was angry that Melissa had been mad at me when I tried to tell her that her father was dying. I was mad at God who I really did not want to talk to anymore. Then, I unplugged a connection to all of my invisible support in order to wallow in my pain, or run from it. Running and wallowing took turns.

Of course, I felt guilty. Being the good co-dependent that I am, guilt came naturally. Wasn't I always disappointing someone? Disappointing myself? Wondering if I could have done better?

Women are born co-dependent. We are trained to take care of others. We spend our lives doing things for other people they are capable of doing for themselves, often crippling them in our over-functioning and allowing them to under-function. I was in the perfect set up for acting out on my co-dependency. I had all the good reasons. My husband was dying. I had to take care of him, make sure he was happy, and make sure he was able to live his last year in the manner he wanted.

However, often I would become tired and angry. Co-dependents do that when they overdo until exhaustion and then start feeling like a victim under the stress. I was not easy to live with many times before and after Pancho died.

"Don't Postpone Your Joy" became my motto. The joy I found was in movement, I just kept moving. In my grief groups, I advised new widows and widowers to take care of themselves. That advice was primarily provided to women. Typically only a few men attended a grief group; one in 10 was average.

One of the activities we would do was to make a list of the 10 most important people in their life. You might want to try that now to get the point. Really…Right now, stop, and write down the 10 most important people in your life.

Now this is the point. Are you on the list? Probably not, that would be selfish, right? Wrong! However, often, when people take care of themselves, especially when they are caregiving, they feel guilt. Guilt is a major part of caregiving and grief. It is a normal reaction and believe me if you do not find one thing to feel guilty about you will find another.

I have heard everything. People feel guilty for denying food, even when their loved one is ready to let go and can no longer swallow, or they believe by giving the prescribed pain medication they killed their loved ones. Most people do the very best they can under the circumstances of caregiving but inevitably guilt is a part of the feelings they are left with when going through grief.

I put on a strong face, as I always did. Soaked in hot baths when I had a chance and chanted mantras (a phrase repeated to aid my concentration during meditation). I used them in an attempt to overcome my fear of what was happening. I wanted to help Pancho have the death he wanted. I was well trained in the philosophy of hospice. He had the right to die with dignity and on his own terms. It was the least I could do.

I had not been the easiest person to live with for almost 40 years, being the headstrong person that I am. I felt like I had been selfish. It was also a part of being a women, it was a part of grief. During the months and years following Pancho's death, the guilt was everpresent. I tried to take care of myself and not feel guilty but it was always lingering in my subconscious.

I coped. Did whatever it took to survive as I advised my clients, "One day at a time, one step at a time." Nevertheless, I could not escape feeling as if I SHOULD be there for other people: my children, my mother, my family. Guilt is unavoidable; it comes with the package. After guilt comes depression, and there was plenty of that to come.

Chapter Twenty-Two:
My Camino of Grief

By spring, I snapped…at everybody.

Like a rabid dog, I kept them at bay by curling my lips and daring them to question my irrationality. I reiterate, my anger was not rational but it did have payoffs. It gave me the energy to prepare to go to the book launch in France. Eventually I threw up my hands. I was leaving. I had been attempting to get things accomplished at the house, including painting inside and out, all the repairs, which had been left undone for years. It was as if a bomb had gone off around me. Everything was in chaos. The living room furniture was stacked in the middle of the room. The yard was cluttered with Pancho's work paraphernalia. I was walking in circles and bumping into walls.

I wanted to get to Europe for May. My mind was as muddled as my house. I could not add a column of numbers to make a bank deposit much less make a clear plan. I was swept along by my days, enduring the thoughts I could not avoid. Elizabeth Palin, my psychic friend from Liverpool, told me she was taking the repositioning cruise from Fort Lauderdale to Southampton. "Escape," I chanted inside my mind. I will leave now I said as I called and talked to an agent who gave me a remarkable fare. I booked it.

When I called Elizabeth with the happy news, she said, to my disappointment, "I didn't mean this April." I knew that. What had I been thinking? I had not been thinking. I had a double cabin on a one-way cruise to Europe by myself. I began to appeal to ALL my family and friends to accompany me. NO takers. I could not believe no one wanted to join me so I told myself, "I'll just go alone."

That was when my friend Michaela jumped onboard. Well, not literally onboard, as she did not want to do the cruise but she would meet me in London and visit the UK. Michaela was a student of *A Course in Miracles* and my loyal sidekick during my retreats and workshops.

My new life goal was to listen for the voice of inner guidance at every crossroad. I had read a book years before called "Listening," written by a student of *A Course in Miracles*. The student decided to spend three months in Europe listening to the voice of the Holy Spirit for guidance. I had always been good at listening to internal guidance, so I decided that is what I would do.

I had friends in England I could visit. I could wander like a gypsy, be blown by the wind, answering to no one. It sounded like a romantic idea, which would have probably been lonely and scary. When Michaela expressed an interest in joining me, I shifted gears.

I went into travel agent mode, booking lodging, renting cars, and making plans. At least it gave me a sense of direction. "Who knows what would have happened to me if I had landed on the shore of Southampton with my bag in hand facing the next month without a plan?" I asked myself. *This* must be the plan. Listening to the Holy Spirit to me meant saying yes to all offers.

Not long after Michaela joined me, another friend, Jill, expressed an interest in visiting France in June. Then a third person said she wanted to go to Italy in July. All of this unexpected activity meant February was full of planning separate tours with my personal focus on Renne le Chateau, and May 10 for the book launch. *The Cathar View: The Mysterious Legacy of Montegur*, would be launched in the tiny village in France made famous by "Holy Blood, Holy Grail" and Henry Lincoln, one of the book contributors.

Once again, I found myself in a scurry of activity. In January, I had minor knee surgery in hopes of mitigating my knee problems and asked to extend my leave from hospice but by February, my supervisor was suspicious that I did not really want to return. I thought I would return. I had all intentions of going back to hospice. The worst part was I felt so bad about letting my co-workers down who had been covering my caseload for months.

It was while attending Jill's Pease's workshop in Vero Beach the decision to retire was made. Jill, an artist trained in a special kind of therapeutic painting, was the woman who wanted to take the Sacred Escape Tour of France in June. While I was in Vero, Cathy, my supervisor from hospice called. She put it on the line, 'It doesn't feel like you want to come back." She nudged me gently. "Well, I guess you are right." I said.

I had already discussed retirement with the Human Resource department at the hospital so I knew I could take early retirement. I resigned that day. My official retirement date would be April 1, 2013 ending my career as a bereavement counselor for hospice. I was no longer supporting the grieving. I was using everything I learned to grieve in the healthiest way I could.

What I did not anticipate was how hard it would be, especially the part about being alone on a cruise full of couples.

I asked Butch, the man whose story I told in "The Cathar View" to stay in the cabin while I was away. When the first copies of "The Cathar View" book arrived from England, I wanted to share one with him. I contacted his sister Mary to locate him. It was perfect timing for both Butch and me. He had an injury from many years of working in the construction industry and was scheduled to have surgery. The cabin behind my house would be a good place for him to recover and he could care for my animals while I was away.

In addition, the Mayan Day Keeper, Dr. Jose Jaramillo, was scheduled to come just prior to my sailing. During his stay, he would perform the sacred fire ceremony and teach us about the continuing impact of the Mayan Calendar on our lives. We had planned his workshop while in Palenque when we had met in December. The first thing he said in the car when Butch and I picked him up from the airport.

"Has it ever occurred to you that we might already be dead?"

"Well, in fact it has." I said.

That sounds bizarre but sometimes it felt to me like we were living in something akin to purgatory and that we were being gently awakened to the idea that we were no longer alive.

In April, 2013 Butch drove me to the port in Fort Lauderdale. I pulled my luggage on board and settled into my dark cabin. The remarkable fare from my travel agent had gotten me an inside cabin on the massive eleven story ship. Was this the what I needed to begin my grief journey? Would England, Iona, Scotland, Findhorn, France, Austria, Italy, and Spain help me get through it?

Alone in my cabin, I asked myself, "Who am I now? Who is beginning this journey?"

Journal:

April 7, 2013: *Alone on a cruise ship beginning a journey that will take me into the future. Thirteen days to cross the Atlantic, Nassau, Puerto Rico, St. Martin and then to South Hampton, meet Michaela.*

The audio journal would prove to be a very helpful healing tool. Answers to my questions began to unravel in conversations with myself as I practiced self-observation. How would I find a place in life again? Pancho was the one who grounded me. I recorded in my journal with myself throughout the trip. I now felt completely alone for the first time.

April 8: *Ate dinner last night, came back to my cabin and got in bed. My cabin is like a little rabbit hole. Woke up in the middle of the night to sounds of my room's TV. I'd left it on for company. The TV person was talking about Pancho, "Heather has a Poncho, Poncho, Poncho," the word describing her favorite outfit sounded out his name repeatedly. You are with me Pancho aren't you? I'm at table 111 with three couples, a French Canadian couple, a couple*

78

from Tennessee, and a couple from the north of England. There is an empty chair beside me. I make them as uncomfortable as I feel. People are actually telling me at five months I should get on with my life. How can they say that?

Back in my cabin, I reviewed the signs I had received in Palenque, the Parrot named Pancho, the waiter named Pancho and more...and meeting Jose the Day keeper. As promised, Jose came to Palm Coast. During his visit, Jose did readings, taught the Mayan Calendar, and ended with a fire ceremony in Pancho's fire pit.

The event took place on the fifth month anniversary of Pancho's death. During the ceremony, we each tossed bundled branches from Pancho's Christmas tree into the fire. I had carefully prepared them for this emotional cleansing ritual. We made other offerings of beans, corn, herbs, coffee, chocolate, and sugar. The fire would carry our gifts to deceased elders and ancestors. It was Pancho's fire. Jose had said the next 13 days were going to be significant for all of us. That was the exact time I would be on the ship. That made me hopeful. It would be a new cycle.

April 10: *Tuesday, third day of cruise....Journal starts with crying. What would it be like if Pancho were with me? I wish they would take the 8thchair away from the table. Elaine, from the north of England, has had melanoma twice and breast cancer. Her story breaks my heart and my story reminds her of death. She and her husband don't eat with us anymore.*

April 15: *Recorded a twenty-two-minute conversation with Renee, the wise and diverse 85-year-old*

79

man. He and his wife, Denise, were from Ontario and we ate together every night. Renee finished reading my Magdalene book while on the cruise. He didn't agree with much of what I had concluded but he did have a message for me.

Renee believes I have a mission and the mission is to form a group of women to change the world, a group of Magdalenes. He believes we should try to reach out to the Pope and that the Catholic Church needs to allow women to be priests. What Renee didn't realize is there is already a group of women all over the world who are working to change the world a little bit everyday by the work of their own lives and in their communities and by connecting with each other. It's not an organized movement and I am just playing out my little part in it. I was flattered by Renee's vision, but the Pope? And women priests? I'm not even Catholic and that seems a stretch. I remembered my favorite quote from A Course in Miracles:

"I am here only to be truly helpful. I am here to represent Him Who sent me. I do not have to worry about what to say or what to do because He Who sent me will direct me. I am content to be wherever He wishes, knowing He goes there with me. I will be healed as I let Him teach me to heal."

That was the best I could do. If I could only get back to those beliefs and live out my life in that manner.

Later on that day I recorded my strange, vivid disjointed dreams and then pontificated aloud:

Maybe I should go to Fatima
Maybe I should stop spending money
Maybe I should get tan
Maybe I should get a massage

Maybe I should remarry
Maybe I should never remarry
Maybe I should sit home just reading and writing
Maybe I should work out and try to get fit
Maybe I should date
Maybe I should never date
Maybe I should sell the house
Maybe I should keep the house
Maybe I should cry
Maybe I should stop crying

"Oh Pancho," I moaned, *"I know we weren't a perfect couple, but it worked for us. Oh, Pancho, do you miss me? Can you miss me? Can you? Can you see me? Was it just our fantasy that you could ride a raindrop, fly into the cosmos, becomes one with the universe? What happened to you? Are you around? Oh Pancho, do you still love me? Oh God, your poor belly, all that you went through, we went through. Was it worth it? At the end, your stomach wasn't bloated, it was flat, and when you lay in that bed and wouldn't get up, you had that naughty little boy look on your face. I had to ask the nurse to put a catheter in and I felt so bad, so guilty. Oh Pancho, I'm so sorry I kept trying to force you to eat. I am sorry I got tired. I have only four days left and I've done nothing toward the book. Can I write the book in four days?*

April 16: *This morning I ended up in the early stretch class and then stayed to do the abs class. In the middle of the night I got up and wandered the ship when everyone else was asleep. It was like a ghost town. I stood on the lower deck looking up through the center of the boat, 11 stories, a floating city with restaurants and shops. I don't know who I am, or where I'm going, or what I believe. Renee says I need to start a movement. It is quite a coincidence we were seated together at table 111.*

Renee, had studied architecture, been a magician, made movies, written a book about Benjamin Franklin, been a bookseller and had owned over 30,000 books. He knows about The Urantia Book and Gurdjieff. It was Renee's 86th birthday. We had small party in their cabin with our odd group, consisting of me, Mr. and Mrs. Conservative America from Tennessee, and Denise, Renee's gentle wife.

After dinner, I found the two widows I'd met, Katherine and Margaret, to say goodbye. I thought of Lily (the Russian woman who I bumped into everywhere I turned on board) and wished she could speak better English so I could hang out with her more.

I took a nap, woke at 11 PM and decided to go for a cup of hot chocolate. I threw a shirt over my long silky pajama pants and, blinded with no contacts, dazed by sleep, ran into Lily again. 3,000 people on board and she was everywhere I turned. She talked me into going to the disco club. Well, actually, I didn't know what she was saying. I just followed her to the disco club, called the Labyrinth, and I danced in my PJ's until I figured a way out. The next day Lily gave me an ice show ticket and showed me her suite (She had been upgraded because her room was next to the morgue). Who knew they had a morgue on a ship?

We watched the show, went for pizza, and laughed. We had fun. I had fun. I wrote one chapter today, 18 pages, and there was a red rose on the table tonight. I should have taken a picture.

82

April 19: I guess it's the 19th, Friday, the last day we cruise. Last night I listened to my recorded talks with Pancho. I listened to his voice from the months before he died, and cried. My phone has been going crazy talking to me. This morning out of nowhere, it "Facetimed" Pancho. No answer. That was weird. I'm scared. I know I didn't pack right. I'm going to have to repack my luggage and leave a whole bag of clothes. I don't know what this trip is about. I don't know what my life is about. I am scared. I'm not sailing across the ocean to go to war. I haven't lost a child. I lost a husband. Pancho always reassured me. "Everything's groovy," he'd say. "Oh Pancho," I sobbed through tears, "Everything's groovy?" I wish that were so.

Chapter Twenty-Three
Southampton to Spain

"Travel is rebellion in its purest form. We follow our hearts. We free ourselves of labels. We lose control willingly. We trade a role for reality. We search for better questions, not answers." Anonymous

This is a reminder, "Don't ever compare your insides with other people's outsides." I pulled my strong positive face back on to show the world, took a deep breath and started portaging. I managed to pare down my luggage until I could pull it off the boat by myself. I was preparing to carry my own bags across Europe.

My next goal was to meet Michaela at Heathrow. We were renting a car and driving it across England. Michaela, a self-proclaimed 'city girl,' recklessly abandoned control and turned her life over to spirit. She promised to live in the moment and trust me to guide her. I was hoping she had made a good choice given my current state of irrationality.

When I first met Michaela, she said, "I will never travel with you after reading your books." She did not like it when I wrote about late nights, arriving at hotels after midnight, and other antics. However, a few years later, when my friend Beth backed out at the last minute on a trip we booked to Spain and France, I called Michaela. "You want to go to

France?" I asked. I was surprised by her answer, "YES! I've been trying to book a trip all day and it just won't work." I gave her the flight information and we took the same flight.

Before we knew it, we were off for our first adventure together. I had promised her we would be all tucked in by dark. I was not able to keep that promise. The first night turned into a fiasco. After flying into Madrid, we drove toward Montserrat to find our hotel. The GPS was not working well. Whoops! It was dark, we were tired. It wasn't the first night I hired a taxi to follow in order to find my way.

We traveled on through Barcelona, to Montsegur, and Rennes Le Chateau, the Cathar sites, and Toulouse. We were pilgrims not tourists. Although we did have a rather short pilgrimage. We visited Lourdes. Michaela walked a bit of the El Camino when we were heading back to Spain. We took a loop trail to find a ceremonial stone seat used by the Knights Templar in Rennes les Bains. While walking up the slightly inclined path, Michaela confessed, "This is the first time I've ever been in the woods."

"What?" I exclaimed. I had spent my life playing in the woods and tracking after Pancho. That is when she told me,

"I grew up in Chicago."

Travelers beware, all trips with Shannon are an adventure, full of magical synchronicities and the unexpected. Nevertheless, I have never lost anyone yet! After that trip, Michaela came with me again on a flight to Paris and a drive that took us all over France, from Paris to the south of France and back up the middle to Chartres Cathedral before flying out.

This would make her third trip with me, once again adventurous. This time Michaela had a slightly emotionally disabled guide. I am not sure I would want to see a review from Michaela on Trip Advisor, but the truth was, I was not okay, far from it. I did my best to put on a happy positive face. When I listened to our conversations on my audio journal, I can hear my 'act as if' strategy as I attempted to reframe any "ants that came to our picnic."

My phone continued to do crazy things, including Facetime people who had died. The next time it happened, I envisioned all my loved ones in heaven holding my grandson. He would soon be born. They were passing him along to Pancho, Dad, Joy, Egan, Mammy (my grandmother) but I had forgotten my brother Tim. I opened my eyes and my phone spontaneously Facetimed Tim. "Oh I'm sorry I forgot you!" I said.

Our rental car was a standard shift, which was no problem. However, I had never driven this model before. I drove all the way to our first food stop when I realized I did not know how to put it in reverse. I asked the first man who walked by and he saved us and we laughed. His son had on a Knight's Templar tunic and carried a sword.

Our first stop was near Stonehenge. There we took the tour. From there we went on to see a variety of spiritual sites. In Glastonbury, I had booked a 'retreat center' within view of the Tor. The Tor is the gigantic mound in the center of the town. The 'retreat center' however turned out to be more of a Bed and Breakfast. By that time, I knew what Michaela preferred. She preferred an American style lodging, often hard to find in the tiny villages. I loved the old and the soulful. I apologized profusely but told her I was sure it was in divine order.

I stepped inside the door to meet Val. Commenting on an East Indian wall hanging I said, "I have a similar one from Puttaparthi, India where I went to see Sai Baba." Val's mouth fell open! "Sai Baba", she exclaimed, "I have seen Baba 7 times! I am a devotee and last week the people who showed up to stay were also devotees!" She was delighted. I went out and told Michaela we were in the right place and we unloaded the car.

It was private, separate from her home and she enlightened us with stories. Her sanctuary was full of crystals and icons from all over the world and every religion. Michaela and I both had some experience with Reiki, the healing modality, Michaela more than I did. We opted to receive the first and second Reiki training from Val while there. Reiki is a Japanese technique of energy healing used to help heal others. Val was a Reiki master and teacher and she passed along the energetic lineage to us through a teaching ceremony. In addition, while staying in her Camelot Retreat Center, we walked up the Tor and around the town of Glastonbury, including Glastonbury Cathedral and the Chalice Well. Val ordered my book, "The Magdalene Awakening: Symbols and Synchronicity Heralding the Re-emergence of the Divine Feminine."

Val told me she had a friend I needed to meet. Through a phone call, I met another author with an interesting story. It was similar to mine. Her book was also about being led on a spiritual adventure by the master numbers. It took her to southern Spain where she bought a convent once inhabited by

Templar Knights. Hilary Carter sent me her book "The 11:11 Code: Secrets of the Convent" on line and I reciprocated.

Michaela and I continued our trip, visiting two more stone circles, Stanton Drew and Avebury. We stopped in Bath to get help fixing my phone. It had continued to misbehave in very strange ways. I wished we had had time to visit the Roman Baths and ruins but by that time, the hole that once existed in our itinerary had been filled. I had not been able to find a place to stay on the island of Iona in Scotland. Elisa, an online spiritual friend, contacted me via email a few days into our trip. She had found a cottage for rent on Iona. Elisa, and I had met on the "The Magdalenes around the World" Facebook site. She was living in Findhorn, Scotland. She herself was an amazing gatherer of people around the world. We arranged to meet Linda, a fourth woman who wanted to share the cottage, before driving to Iona. In Bath, I was able to transfer the money to the owner of the cottage and then continued driving north.

I took Michaela to the Pheasant Inn in Bassenthwaite, the same Inn Dr. Arthur Guirdham wrote about when sharing his story of a group incarnation of Cathars. The Cathars were medieval primitive Christians exterminated by the Catholic Church during the Albigensian Crusade. "The Cathar View" was written about the same group. Dr. Guirdham and his books had played a significant part in the Cathar story unfolding in my life. We then drove on to an estate home in Temple Sowerby, Acorn Banks Estates, which is one of the oldest remains of a Templar Commandery in England.

I had first heard of Temple Sowerby while living in Cornwall when I was 29 years old. I had tried to find it for years. Eventually I visited it in 2001. That was before it had been sold to the National Trust. Michaela and I were able to tour the house and visit the room I had written a story about in 1985. It was a true story about a dream. The story had been told to me by Molly Worth. The reoccuring dream had visited her in 1942. She told it to me while I was living in England in 1982 and I had recorded it. The director of the trust house was interested in hearing the mysterious story. I promised to email her a recounting of Molly's dream about the room in Acorn Banks when I returned home.

Spring in England is the most delightful time of the year. We enjoyed an English tea and cake at 4:44 PM. I noticed the time on the Grandfather clock that ticked next to us. The garden on the property was full of blue bells and daffodils. From Temple Sowerby, we drove to Roslyn Chapel to meet Linda. It happened to be the first night Roslyn Chapel opened for a candlelight evening of poetry written by local poets. They were accompanied by a three-piece ensemble including cello and violins. Roslyn Chapel, poetry, music, candles and moonlight provided an enchanting opportunity.

Michaela, Linda, and I drove on to Iona, via Mull and the ferries. There are two ferries to get to Iona. One takes you from Oban to Mull and the trip takes a couple of hours. The other is a short ride from Mull to Iona. We arrived to cold weather and drizzling rain, a few more "ants in our picnic." I had bumped into a rock, denting the car. "It's only a bit of metal" one woman said reassuringly as we looked at the damage.

Nevertheless, that required insurance reports and more aggravation for me.

When the ferry arrived on Iona, we had a long walk pulling our luggage up the lanes. We were wet and chilled to the bone. There are only a few cars on Iona and those are only for residents. We started dragging our roller bags and backpacks up the hill to the cottage we had rented where Elisa was waiting. A kind man passing by in a car offered to help and he directed us to our cottage.

Elisa stood at the gate to greet us. It was a very typical example of accommodations on the island. It was charming but unfortunately, for Michaela it was a very old, damp cottage, with one bathroom on the first floor and a stairway with shallow steps winding upstairs. It had a small coal-burning fireplace in the sitting room. I let the others have the bedrooms upstairs and chose to keep the coal fire burning throughout our stay. I slept on the couch.

It was a very cold, rainy, windy spring in Scotland and because we had to take the cottage for the entire week on Iona that meant Michaela would not make it to Findhorn. She also did not have enough time to take a tour of Ireland at the end of her trip. She wanted to take a tour before flying out of Dublin. In my distracted state, I did not realize the extent of her disappointment. I was focusing on myself, selfishly. My grandson would be born that week. It was an emotional moment in my life. I was feeling very torn. This was a pilgrimage and I knew challenges.

We are told we should be Pilgrims in life, but instead we behave like tourists. Pilgrims are on a special journey. Every part of that journey has special meaning; the setbacks, the frustrations, as well as the joys. Tourists are out to enjoy life, to seek pleasure, fun and just rest. Pilgrims carry little with them, just enough for their needs. Tourists are burdened with possessions and are always anxious about losing them. Pilgrims stay as long as they need to be in a place. Tourists have schedules to keep and are always rushing. Pilgrims are humble, open to people, and experiences. Tourists are arrogant, they know what they want, and they'll find it, see it, do it. Pilgrims share what they have. Tourists never have quite enough. Pilgrims are changed by their journey. Tourists are always a little bit disappointed. It's never quite as good as they had hoped. Lord let us be Pilgrims in life, not just Tourists. That trip confirmed our status as Pilgrims; we had ample opportunities for learning.

The baby would be born on April 28, and I would not be there. In my normal state of mind, I would have been able to fit it all in, fix it, I would have planned better, done better but I was far from normal. The nice thing was the week was filled with a warm comradery of women sharing kitchen chores and cooking and life stories. Each of us brought an entirely different path arriving in similar ports of call. Mary Magdalene and Archangel Michael were both part of our shared stories. In addition, apparently the owner of the cottage was connected to Mary Magdalene (as is the isle of Iona by legend and history). One night while I was drying the dishes, I stopped to look more closely at a sterling silver souvenir spoon someone had used for their tea. It said Mary Magdalene. We all identified strongly with the archetype of Mary Magdalene, the consummate strong, spiritual woman on a mission to bring back the voice of the divine feminine. Iona was filled with more miracles. With the baby's birth on the horizon, we discussed Grand- mothering. *What did I want to be called* they wanted to know? He would arrive while we were on the island. Michaela, an experienced Grandmother, said I should decide now so as not to be called some crazy name the baby chose.

It was a bittersweet time for me; letting go of my adult children, rejoicing for the birth of our first grandchild, and missing Pancho. He could not be there for his birth either. Pancho's giant smile when he heard the results of the ultrasound is imprinted in my mind. The baby was a boy and they would name him William, after Pancho and Treve. I showed Pancho the picture of the ultrasound on my phone. He held it in his hands all day dreaming of our grandson Finn he would never meet. Pancho was William Clark, Treve was William Treve, now Finn our grandson would be William Gerald Finn Andersen. It broke both our hearts knowing Pancho would never hold him in his arms. I took comfort in the image Elizabeth Palin had given me, "The dead loved ones hold the babies before they come to us.," she said. I hoped so much that Pancho had Finn in his arms. I closed my eyes to imagine that once more.

Page was having C-section, which meant we knew when the baby would be born. My sister Lissa, Beth, and my mother drove to Daytona Beach that day. I spent the time talking to Pancho. "Pancho," I said, "Send me a sign you know about the birth. Send me a rainbow." All day long, I looked for a rainbow. Not likely, since on Iona, April 28, 2013, was another rainy, cold, dreary day. I busied myself with my job as fire tender. I had quickly learned to maintain a coal fire in the small brick fireplace. At 4:44 AM Page's mother sent me a picture of Finn! I looked at his little face all day. I made his picture my screensaver. In the late afternoon, we walked down to Iona Cathedral and the hotel where we were able to use Wi-Fi to see all of the pictures sent to my email.

Confused and sad, I wanted Pancho's signature rainbow! It was so important for me to know Pancho was aware of his grandson's birth. The weather did not help. Iona is spectacular in all her moods but spring is a season of damp, misty days. Spring brings mushrooms, fresh grass, flowers, and baby lambs. They are everywhere. I had never seen the season of lambing. Across all the pastures, tiny black and white babies pranced in the fields. Occasionally, they escaped through holes in the fences. Then the lambs dash up and down the roads causing havoc. Finn was born during the season of the lambs.

As we were leaving the hotel, I looked over my left shoulder. For a split second, a rainbow appeared. Quickly, I took a picture. On my phone's screensaver, the one with the newborn face of little Finn, I saw the time, 6:22! Those numbers represented the date of Pancho's birthday. I captured his time with the newborn's face by taking a screenshot on my phone. I believed Pancho knew that Finn had arrived. The rainbow told me he knew. I had prayed for assurances. The numbers said, "Yes, it's me." The rainbow said, "Yes, it's me." That made it a double hit. It was a clear message with an exclamation point! A surge of elation filled my heart.

May fifth was a bright, sunny day. We all gathered in the grass to celebrate Wesak (Buddha's birthday.) We played with the baby lambs, walked on the beach, and picked up green serpentine pebbles. Iona is famous for these unique green stones. From the island, we made a trip to Kilgore where the stained glass window of Jesus alongside a pregnant Mary Magdalene.

It was time to leave Iona. Flight reservations were made from Edinburgh to Barcelona where I would meet Jill on June 6 for her tour of Spain and France. I booked a hotel close to the Edinburgh airport so I could turn in the car and walk back. Michaela had flown out to Dublin the previous day. I embraced the day as an opportunity to sleep late, recover and regroup.

The third woman I was to take on tour to Italy canceled the trip because her mother was placed on hospice. In truth, I was relieved. Now that time was vacant. What would I do after Jill flew home? Could I embrace this space as opportunity to be in the moment, turn the future over to the Holy Spirit, and follow its guidance?

Sitting at the Edinburgh airport, waiting for my flight with a coffee in front of me, I glanced up at the decorations hanging high above. Surfboards! Did I see surfboards? Not just surfboards, but longboards, the type of surfboard Pancho rode. How can that be in Edinburgh, Scotland? Is this another sign from you, Pancho? Perhaps Pancho was letting me know, <u>everything is groovy</u>.

Chapter Twenty-Four
Tortilla to Croissants

I arrived in Barcelona a day before Jill and caught a bus downtown to find the Apple Store. I felt comfortable driving on the French roads, but not as much in Spain, because of a little PTS due to the challenging experience with the GPS while traveling with Michaela. We had gotten lost in Barcelona and I just did not have the energy to face the GPS alone. I enjoy having a navigator next to me. My French was better than my Spanish. I spoke Spanish with a French accent and I could not easily make the transition coming from Scotland where I was not sure we were speaking the same language at times. My phone had gone completely wacko. Without a working phone, GPS included, I felt handicapped. I wanted to be very sure everything was in order before Jill arrived. The Apple Store people were nice enough to give me a quick fix for my phone. They warned it needed some serious attention when I returned home.

Once again, I booked a hotel at Montserrat and stayed alone the first night. In the morning, I drove to the airport and there when Jill arrived. Jill and I stayed a few days at Montserrat to combat her jetlag. She was a wonderful sport, happy to do and see whatever came up. We visited the black mountains that erupted on the horizon as we approached and admired the beautiful Black Madonna of Montserrat.

The route we took from Spain to France was the one Kathleen McGowan suggested in her books. The last survivors of the massacre at Montsegur had taken the route, supposedly carrying a treasure. As we drove, we listened to segments of Kathleen's books, which pertained to the Cathar history. Her books are fiction but are believed to hold many truths. The Spanish/French segment of this Sacred Escape had a focus on Rennes le Chateau for the book signing.

Jill and I drove straight to the Cathar mountain, Montsegur. We checked in at a Gite de France (Bed & Breakfast). It was owned by friends I had made over the years, Yves and Nicole Masset. They owned a home and their Gite de France sits at the foot of the mysterious legendary mountain. This was my tenth trip to the magical mountain.

From there we drove to Rennes le Chateau. The winding road up the mountain to the tiny village of Rennes le Chateau had changed so much since my first trip in 1999. Now, there were parking lots for tour buses. Because I was familiar with the village, I drove straight to the top and found a parking place. The book event took place in Le Jardin de Marie, a restaurant in the village made famous by Henry Lincoln and Michael Baigent in their book, *Holy Blood, Holy Grail*.

There were 25 people gathered. Ani Williams, another one of the contributors to *The Cathar View*, played her harp and accompanied Henry Lincoln in a reading from *The Cathar View*. It was one of his poems called: *There is a Time for Burning*. We each stood briefly and shared a bit about our chapter in the compendium. Then we gathered for a meal and toasted with champagne before Jill and I went back to explore the village of Montsegur. The village was built in the shadow of the famous Cathar mountain.

While in the Languedoc region of southern France, *le Pays Cathare* (meaning Cathar country), Jill and I went to stay a few days with Colum Hayward the publisher, Dave Patrick, the book's editor, and another friend, Elizabeth. They were staying in a region of Languedoc, famous for its Cathar caves. Colum took us along paths and into a number of caves and we watched as young men scaled surrounding cliffs. On the walk he said, "I know only one other person who lives in Florida. Do you know Pearl Rauberts?" "No." I replied and then I paused, "Wait a minute. I do know a Pearl Rauberts!" Her telephone number was on my cell phone. I talked to her once when I was booking Grandfather Rick, a Native American speaker teaching Lakota ceremony. I think she was in south Florida. "She used to be my secretary in the London Lodge," Colum added. What could I say? It happens all the time, all over the world; circles within circles of synchronicity. Countless occurrences such as this have convinced me - we meet soul family wherever we go. After traveling the world and finding connections to people in Hong Kong and Australia, South America, and Paris to name a few, I began to believe we come to earth with a group of spiritual time travelers and meet to exchange lessons, lifetime after lifetime. Perhaps it is true that we exist as a pod of souls with a shared experience on earth and perhaps beyond. If you can think of an organ and the cells that come together to make it up, each of us and our

97

"parallel lives" come together to create a family with whom we share a mission and perhaps we ascend together leaving the cycle of reincarnations when we've all accomplished our shared tasks.

Much of our time in France was left open for flexibility. We did secure a hotel in Arles for 3 days around the dates of the Gypsy Festival at St. Marie de la Mer. The first part of trip focused on Cathars, Mary Magdalene and Black Madonnas. The second part focused on art, shopping, and Provence.

Kathleen McGowan, the author of *The Expected One* and other Magdalene novels, was in the area with a tour. It was only months since Pancho and her husband Filip had both died. We appeared to be dealing with our grief in a similar way, not staying still. I ran into Kathleen three different times including at the Gypsy festival, Carcassonne, and Rennes le Chateau. She invited us to join their group but Jill was ready to move on. We headed for the tiny village of La Maurine where her artist friend taught classes.

There were a few dreary days of rain but in the picturesque village, who could complain? We ate and drank, Jill shopped, and I saw another rainbow. We crammed a massive amount of travel into our 3 weeks, driving through Spain, the Languedoc, Provence and the coast of Brava. We were in Cannes during the week of the film festival, where we struggled to find some accommodations. A Policeman sent us in the direction to find a Gite du France. We found a safe Villa overlooking Grasse, a village known for its perfume and candy production. We visited a candy factory.

Another book event was held at Watkins's Book, the oldest, most famous metaphysical bookshop in London. This event occurred in the middle of our trip so while Jill stayed in Arles, I flew from Nantes to London. I spent one night with friends in London and participated in the book signing featuring *The Cathar View.* I flew back to Arles 48 hours later. After the book event, Colum and Dave took me in a cab to the bus station. Around midnight I caught the coach to the airport. I flew all night to be back to pick up Jill for the first day at St. Marie de la Mer's celebration of The Three Marys' and St. Sarah.

We arrived a day before the masses of people descended. Jill loved the gypsy festival, the women in bright, frilly dresses and little girls dancing in circles with their arms in the air. We visited the church and its underground vault thick with smoke from the candles lit for Sarah, the black Madonna. We drove past the pink Flamingos and white horses of the Camargue region. From there it was back down the coast of Brava where we spent couple of nights in a hotel on the Mediterranean south of Barcelona. I delivered Jill safely to the airport and turned in the car. Taking a deep breath, I asked myself, "What next?"

Chapter Twenty-Five:
Listening

What was next? That was the question on the table. I had been distracted from my grief by other peoples' needs. Now I was alone for the first time since I had stepped off the boat. I did not know what to do. My plan was to follow inner guidance, live in the moment, without fear. I wanted to stay in Europe and meet Melissa in July. I had no ticket home so it was the perfect opportunity to listen.

I had an invitation from friends who lived in Austria. They invited me to visit. Brigitte had been visiting her home in Florida most winters throughout Pancho's illness and had helped us learn a variety of healing modalities, including good nutrition. She had performed spiritual healing on him as well. She understood my loss. In addition, Elisa had invited me back to Scotland, and Dave Patrick suggested we could do a workshop in Nairne not far from Findhorn.

I accepted both offers. The day after Jill left, I formulated a plan. I bought a train ticket through Germany and a plane ticket to Scotland. The weather continued to be severe the summer of 2013. On the way to Austria, my train had to be diverted due to floods in the Danube. It continued to rain in Austria but Brigitte happily took me to the small towns around her village. She took me for walks in the hills around her house, to the peaks in Italy just across the border from Austria, and to a medieval castle not far from her home. We shared conversation, wine, and whole foods.

I looked forward to seeing her again in Florida and said goodbye. In Edinburgh I rented a lime green VW Beetle. In it, I drove north to meet Dave Patrick in Nairne. From there I found Elisa in the little cottage on the perimeter of the Findhorn community. She showed me around and explained the history and politics of Findhorn. I only knew of it through the book "The Magic of Findhorn" by Paul Hawken.

The founders of Findhorn made a garden out of rocky soil and it exists still as a thriving spiritual community, unlike any other in the world. The days at Findhorn were peaceful. However, I had a UTI, a stomach virus, and a broken tooth. Physically, I was challenged. Sometimes physical pain diverts our attention from emotional pain, another way to avoid grief.

Dave Patrick and I conducted the workshop in a small town outside of Findhorn. I performed a ceremony initiating attendees into the Virtual Order of the Knights Templar using a genuine Scottish Sword. A case of books had been sent to Dave and Dave found homes for most of the books in Scotland, France, and Spain. My books were becoming cairns, trail markers for like-minded thinkers to find and follow. I love hearing tales of how readers find my book, and their connections and synchronicities with the story.

Elisa and I decided to drive to Spain. We booked a ferry. Somehow, we showed up in the wrong town, ready to load on the wrong boat. It was as if there was a magnet pulling me to Plymouth, instead of Portsmouth. Plymouth was the first place Pancho held his son when returning from Galatia to England when Treve was one month old. Elisa and I located the place to turn in the rental car and we were dropped off at the ferry station. Unfortunately, it was the wrong port.

"No, it can't be!" I said, aghast. We expected to travel all the way to the northwest coast of Spain but traded our tickets for a shorter route to Roscoff, on the northern coast of France. My strategy was to follow guidance. Guidance took me to places precious to Pancho and me. With no forethought, I was taken through Nice and Cannes, St. Tropez. Pancho proposed to me there in our early 20s. Later I ended up in Biarritz. We had been together there in 2005 on our last European trip together.

I adopted an 'all is in divine order' attitude, operating from a fog of grief. Distracted and often confused, I cried quietly in moments when grief was triggered, but my companions genuinely understood. They flowed with our guidance embracing the grand adventure.

We rented a car the next morning. The port was tiny, the rains torrential. We started driving. "Where now?" An entirely new trip route led us to visit the standing stones at Carnac, then Chartres Cathedral. We arrived in Chartres on a Friday. My trips to France were frequently built around Friday in Chartres when the labyrinth was available to walk. I walked the labyrinth, and attended mass. I actually took communion, something I fear Catholic readers might have an issue with, but Michaela, a self-proclaimed "recovering Catholic" encouraged me to do so the last time we had visited. I courageously participated in the ritual at Chartres secretly wondering if I would not be struck down by an angry God. I was not. The God I knew was all about love and so I believed had no objection.

The labyrinth represents a pilgrimage for those who could not make the journey on the most famous pilgrimage, the El Camino. Both are traditional expressions of grief. That day, the labyrinth was crowded. I entered the Cathedral and stood in line. It was a 40-minute walk. My Kleenex was soggy and in a tiny knot at the end. Walking into the center, I relived my life with Pancho. In the center, I checked into the moment, and walking out, I attempted to envision a life without Pancho. It was easy to "forget" he would not be there when I returned home. I had committed to stay until July to meet Melissa in Biarritz, France.

Chapter Twenty-Six:
Crossing the Border into Spain -Lightning and Floods

Elisa and I drove through France visiting some of the Magdalene and Cathar sites. The last location we stopped was a church Fillip Coppens identified as The Chartres of the Templar. It continued to rain, but the bottom dropped out when we left the cathedral to cross the border into Spain. Lightning struck followed by booming claps of thunder. We drove alongside a muddy river, the rushing water overflowing its banks. Elisa cringed, but I kept driving fearlessly.

We traveled until almost dark and stopped at a roadside hotel. It seemed to be a trucker's stop. The television played while we ate and watched the news coverage of the villages we just passed crumbling into the currents. The following morning, we continued driving. We stopped at the Alhambra and arrived in Nerja.

Nerja, a pristine village of stacked white houses and colorful people, was graced by blue green Mediterranean waters, and palm trees. Three cats occupied the house Elisa watched for a member of the Findhorn community. The owner possessed two homes, one cottage in Findhorn and one in Nerja. They had been swapping locations for several years.

Nerja provided excellent time to rest following the rapid pace of summer. Several days I slept until noon, and took naps. The sun was blistering, the breeze brisk. We walked into the town full of summer vacationers, happy people, and children playing. On the beach, I collected small, flat, perfectly round stones created by the gentle roll of waves at the edge of the sea.

Outside the perimeter of the village, were underground caverns with their majestic stalactites and stalagmites. Driving down a winding dirt road running along the sea, I saw a hand painted sign that said 'Yoga.' "Look Elisa, Yoga!" I said excitedly, and we drove to explore further.

There we met a retired professional ballerina from Paris. She lived in the rustic retreat built by her boyfriend. It was built on a hill, and it overlooked the Mediterranean. Her family included two Ukrainian children, victims of war and abuse. Her French accent charmed us and we were welcomed with an embrace. Pictures of Sai Baba hung on her walls. She, like Val in Glastonbury, was a devotee and she wanted to share the story of being healed by Baba. The following week a Swami from India was arriving, but it was time for me to move on.

I left Elisa and drove north through central Spain. Because I had rented the car in France, I wanted to return it in France. Biarritz was the perfect place to meet Melissa. I had never driven the central route in Spain so I enjoyed landscape I had never seen. Spain was much more beautiful than I had imagined. It had spectacular mountains, seasides and flatland desserts. It took two long days and one night to reach France. There I checked into a hotel near the airport and planned to pick up Melissa the following day.

It was the end of June. I could not wait to see her. As I mentioned, anger had afflicted our family and we had all gone to our separate corners to grieve. I understood anger was normal and allowed my own. I tried not to be hurt by theirs. They had a right to grieve in their own way but we were all hurting. We were mad Pancho was gone from our lives. We each acted out our own drama of mourning.

My grief pilgrimage had taken me over 5000 km in three months. I knew I had to go home at some point. Most of all, I wanted to meet Finn, my new grandbaby. What I did not want was to face the empty side of the bed.

Chapter Twenty-Seven
Santiago

Melissa had left just after Pancho's death and just before her 29th birthday. We coped in a similar manner, sought out changing landscapes. Flying to different corners of the world, we crisscrossed the planet, meeting in places, but moving in opposite directions.

Between the two of us, we traveled to more than 20 countries the first years following Pancho's death. Nine months after his death, we met in Biarritz to begin dealing with our mutual loss. It was time to move toward reconciliation.

A road in Spain lay ahead for Melissa, the El Camino de Santiago. She had found a way to honor her father. The walk offered a place to examine her emotional pain by pushing herself through the physical pain. The road is also known as "the way of the stars." It is a pilgrim's route taking sojourners under the Milky Way galaxy.

The ancient religious/spiritual pilgrimage was walked by kings and princes, knights and paupers, men and women. Trails leading to the El Camino sprawl across the map originating from numerous European cathedrals. The culminating point is found in one sacred location in the northwest corner of Spain in

Galatia. That is location of the Cathedral dedicated to San Jacque in the town of Santiago de Compostella.

Melissa joined others pilgrims in the 800-year-old tradition used for expressing grief in a tangible way. The rewards of the Camino are a passport full of stamps, a mass, a certificate and the promise of an inner transformation few could describe unless they too tread the path. This unique undertaking advances progress physically, spiritually, and culturally, while providing an opportunity for self-reflection. Its dramatic scenery crosses the Pyrenees Mountains to Pamplona and Burgos and through Sarria. Honored as a World Heritage Site the pilgrimage trades blisters and tired, calloused feet in for an opened heart, and a changed inner landscape.

I was introduced to the El Camino by Shirley MacLaine's book, *The Camino*. The best-known segment is over 500 miles (740 kilometers). By 2011, I understood the pilgrimage could serve as as a tool for mourning a death. At times during my work with hospice clients, I had shown the movie, *The Way,* produced by and featuring Martin Sheen and Emilio Estevez demonstrating the grief journey. Shirley MacLaine's book and Martin Sheen's movie had popularized the pilgrimage. Pancho and I saw the movie together the year before he died.

Melissa chose this offering to her father because it was significant to him as well. In 2005, Pancho packed a surfboard and flew to Spain with Beth and me. I had invited him to join us on our sacred escape enticing him with stories of surf off the coast of France. Beth and I had been making plans for the trip for years. We sought an inner initiation. Pancho was hoping for surf.

When we watched "The Way" 9 years after his first diagnosis of stage 4 cancer, I envisioned walking the Camino again, *for* Pancho. We had had years of doctor's visits, hospitals, biopsies, chemotherapy, radiation, wheat grass, juicing, mind control, exercise, hope and bad news. Those years prepared us for the end. We were as prepared as one can be for our ultimate physical separation.

When the inevitable came to pass and Pancho died, I was 60. I had a bad knee. My first knee surgery was in January 2013 only months after he died. I believed I would be incapable of taking the pilgrimage in his memory, but Melissa picked up the baton. In July 2013, Melissa and I were on a mission to honor Pancho. I picked her up at the small airport in southeast corner of France. Melissa had flown in from Croatia, Bulgaria, via London. We chose Biarritz. It was only a short distance from the most famous jumping off point of the Camino, St. Jean Pied de Port.

Melissa and I had not seen each other for months, our relationship strained by our mutual loss. Somehow, we had found comfort in new places, new people, and old friends rather than each other. She was a welcomed sight, encumbered by her large backpack and smiling face. She tossed her cumbersome bundle into the backseat of the rental car at the airport and kissed my cheek in greeting.

By morning, she was complaining of a severe sore throat. Undaunted she moved ahead with her planned itinerary. She was going to walk the Camino and she was going to start it on July 1! We made an appointment with a doctor and by 10:00 AM Melissa began her journey representing both of us. I was concerned about her starting out with Strep throat but had no influence.

We bought antibiotics and picked up a Camino passport. The official office was in St. Jean Pied de Port. The lane leading up to the office was lined with shops. They sported Camino paraphernalia, some symbolic and some necessary, from scallop shells to walking sticks and backpacks. We bought a scallop shell (pilgrim's wear this symbol) and tied it onto Melissa's backpack. Walking down the ancient, narrow, cobblestone road, I took short measured steps nursing my knee. Our shared adventure began.

We did not talk about Pancho; not right away. It was still too raw. I tried to remember Pancho's admonitions from the last months, "just be and listen." At the foot of the stone gates, the path led out of town and onto the trail. It was there we found the first of the yellow markers for Melissa to follow. She began the first leg, a long one, climbing up and over the Pyrenees Mountains.

The leg from St. Jean Pied de Port to Roncesvalles was extreme. As Melissa walked away waving, I took her picture, the first of many. Alone in the town, I wandered through the shops full of souvenirs, hats, and supplies. It was market day and the streets were lined with booths full of everything imaginable from colorful dresses and purses, to kitchenwares and sweets. I walked by the river where some pilgrims were camping and finally bought a walking stick to give Melissa at the end of the day. I inscribed "Pancho" and the dates of his birth and death onto the shank. My plan was to accompany her for the first few legs, drive ahead, find a hostel or albergues and walk back up the trail to meet her.

I drove to Roncesvalles. We had visited the village by car the day before on June 31 when we shared our first pilgrim's meal. There was a 5-star hotel available. I booked it for the evening of July 1. Ahead, Melissa would be staying in modest rooms provided for the pilgrims. Those accommodations were inexpensive, available along the entire route, and they usually offered a meal of bread, wine, and a main course to welcome pilgrims at the end of the day.

On that first day, we had agreed to meet at the hotel. I arrived early and walked back up the hill to the edge of the trail to look for Melissa. I chased a few yellow butterflies with my camera. Somehow, we missed each other and Melissa called from the hotel. She had made the day's walk in amazing time. It was so early we had to wait until dinner was being served.

In the hotel, we showered and repacked our bags. The first days I carried a portion of her things in the car. We inquired at the hotel desk about having some of her things sent ahead to her final destination. She was going on from Santiago to meet friends in Corsica and needed a different wardrobe. We discovered you could choose to have your bags sent ahead each night if you could not bear the weight. Melissa preferred to carry her pack.

Her backpack was brimming. I carried it down the elevator just to see what it felt like to carry the weight. I carried no weight myself when I began my routine of walking backwards up the trail to meet Melissa at the end of the day. The second evening I arrived early and began walking back up the trail. I had only been walking a short distance when I saw her coming over a small stone bridge crossing the river. She was

111

smiling and chatting with a tall lean young man who spoke broken English.

Melissa introduced us and then together we walked to the edge of the river where a group of multicultural pilgrims lounged on the grass under a shade tree. Melissa slid into the cold river fully clothed. After her brief swim, we continued to our small hotel. It was a step down from the previous night. We shared a pitcher of local wine with an Irish couple.

The third night, we stayed at an official albergue high atop a hill in an ancient village. I arrived early, about 11am, and was welcomed into a private room with a double bed and its own bathroom. I was surprised by the comfort at the Albergue. Our window opened up on the courtyard of a Cathedral and the bell in the tower rang every 15 minutes. It clanged out the time all day and all night. Was it to help the pilgrims find their way? It may have been intended to be welcoming, but proved to make sleeping a challenge.

Once again, I acted as her photographer, this time as Melissa arrived. She posed in front of the church before our meal. We ate dinner around a table with a group of handsome, bright, young men, mostly college age and all traveling alone. Large bowls heaping with spaghetti, green salads, and loaves of homemade bread were passed around as everyone shared food and stories. Later, we wandered into a petite shop looking at strange selections on the shelf and in the cooler case. Melissa found some food for her pack. She did not stir that night, despite the clanging alarm, and she set off early the next morning.

Mountainous roads began to turn into flat terrain and golden wheat fields. As I drove, the landscape stirred my memory. I had driven along the same roads I with Beth, Pancho and his surfboard. Beth and I had traveled to France and Spain with the intention of walking 111 km of the Camino, from Sarria to Santiago de Compostella. It was the shortest segment for which you could be deemed "official pilgrims." Even though we were driving, we stopped along the way to have our pilgrim's passport stamped at the cathedrals or shops in the little villages. Our passport stamped out proof of our journey as we drove from St. John Pied la Port to start our walk in Sarria.

Our destination was the Cathedral in Santiago de Compostella and the pilgrim's mass; we were not able to earn the official certificate without completing the walk on foot. Beth and I had been training for the walk for more than a year. She had excitedly written to me in an email:

"Shannon, I looked up the El Camino and found a map of the pilgrimage route to Santiago de Compostella Camino and saw that it starts in France, goes across the Pyrenees, and continues its way east to west across northern Spain. The map gives all the little villages along the route. Of course, I am thinking the town mentioned in your book is right on the route. I cannot remember the town's name. Anyway, then I went to the library and checked out Shirley MacLaine's book. I wanted to read you the Introduction, but I will just type the part that excited me: It said that the "Camino" Road - or "The Way" lies directly under the Milky Way and follows the ley lines that reflect the energy from those star systems above it. The energy of the ley lines increases the rate of vibration of the etheric and dense matter that makes up the human brain. The result of this stimulation is the production of more full, conscious awareness and information that was previously repressed. This can be disturbing and frightening because it means that through this energy one becomes a more psychic being." Now, I do not know about you, but I think this is definitely synchronistic...the Camino (which I have been very drawn to and interested in), and your desire to go to the Pyrenees are intertwined. In addition, what about the ley lines making you more psychic? So, are we supposed to go?

We agreed. We did want to go. In 2005, we spent every weekend walking 5 to 6 miles breaking in our feet and shoes. Pancho planned to escort us with the car (as I did for Melissa) but it did not happen that way. When we arrived, Beth was ill. In Sarria, she checked into a hotel to recuperate. Pancho and I decided to make the first 22.5 km leg together. I personally believe the leg from Sarria to Porto Marin, a 22.5 km leg, was one of the nicest of the pilgrimage. If I brought a group back to sample the journey that would be the leg I would choose.

The night before we left, Pancho and I bought a walking stick. We each had our scallop shell from home. We hung them from our fanny packs stuffed with granola bars and water. There was a mass in the church in Sarria to receive a blessing. We were, hoping for a miraculous cure for Pancho. The morning we left, we caught a taxi from the hotel to the yellow arrows and stone scallop shells marking the path. That taxi, I took note, had a '444' car tag, one of the master numbers significant for me.

It took all day for Pancho and I to walk the leg, passing wandering cows, wild Calla lilies, peasants working in their fields, giant oaks, stone bridges, lady

114

bugs sunning on bright green leaves along the well-worn path with only a few other pilgrims. Pancho, though he had cancer, was very fit. At home, he worked hard on his clam lease, surfed and fished, rode his bike or ran and had no need of the training Beth and I had endured.

It was nearing sunset when Pancho and I arrived at the hotel Beth had booked months before. We were very appreciative. We soaked our blistered feet in a hot bath, drank a bottle of wine and went down for our meal of bright yellow paella with fresh shrimp and clams. Afterwards we fell into bed and slept soundly. The following morning a taxi came to retrace our steps in order to meet Beth at the hotel. The taxi, a different one, had a 444 car tag! I took a picture, as always, capturing synchronicities. I was still in awe of such unusual coincidences. I wanted a complete record of our journey.

Beth was still sick. She had a nasty cold. In a couple of days, she felt better. I convinced her to walk back up the trail from a mid-point on one of the legs. The walk was supposed to be short enough to return to our car and the hotel in one day. "You can't come all this way and not walk a portion of the pilgrimage," I told her. It was supposed to be easy, about a 6 km walk (12 km roundtrip) but because of me, it turned into a real fiasco.

We started walking up the path past pilgrims, "backwards." I had taken the lead following the yellow arrows in reverse and the road soon found us on hilly terrain with no other pilgrims. We kept walking; we kept climbing, and climbing, and climbing. Pancho and I wanted to stop and rest but Beth was so worried about getting a meal or running out of energy that she would not stop. She now took the lead and I was dragging behind.

It was growing late and the sun was sinking when we found ourselves standing at a marker announcing we were at 6,000 meters. A pedestrian walked by. He expressed concern about our being able to reach the trail again before dark. The mountains had turned dusty pink and hazy. That increased our pace. We were moving only on instinct with no idea where we were but we had figured out I had taken the bike route marked by yellow arrows painted on the road. I was in trouble!

We came to a crossroad giving us the option of taking three directions. Which way now? I saw a house off in the distance and started to move in that direction when a bus came over the hill. Beth and Pancho stood in the middle of the road waving their waking sticks. Beth climbed on the empty bus and tried to convey our dilemma to the driver. He pointed toward the road that would take us back to the Camino but feeling sorry for us motioned for us to come onboard. He drove 20 minutes out of his way to deliver us.

After the drive up and around curving hilly roads, he dropped us off at the official trail. We climbed off the bus, still not sure where we were but very appreciative. It turned out that we were being watched over in extraordinary ways, because, he dropped us off *exactly* where we had started that morning. It was across the street from the hotel where we had booked a room and left our car. What a relief!

We opted to drive into Santiago the next day and tour the Cathedral. We were completing the tradition of knocking our brow on the pillar of wisdom and visiting the golden statue of St. Jacque. Afterwards, we drove the beautiful northern segment of the loop back to the St. Jean Pied de Port. It was a modern pilgrim's tour, in a car.

On my tour with Melissa, I was driving, not walking the Camino. That is, except when I walked 3 to 4 km back up the trail to meet her at the end of the day. I stayed several more nights. I told her I was going to be 'walking backwards' to meet her. She, knowing the quirkiness of her mother did not say anything until a few days later when she said, "You better be careful walking backwards. You could hurt your knee."

She had envisioned me literally walking backwards. That certainly would have been an awkward way to complete the pilgrimage but she thought it must be some kind of weird spiritual gesture. "No, I'm not literally walking backwards!" I corrected. "I am just walking back up the trail to meet you." We both laughed.

Walking backwards on the El Camino is actually a perfect metaphor for grief. It is a pilgrimage. There are no arrows pointing you in the right direction. You feel lost, blind, stumbling, slow, and awkward; and for both, grief and walking the Camino, a spiritual gesture is a part of the journey requiring heart and courage. Those around me who knew I had been helping people grieve for over 12 years as a hospice bereavement counselor, expected me, to complete the experience with at least, some kind of educated ease. Even I naively thought I was prepared, strong and capable. I gathered within myself the bravado thinking I was "ready."

I convinced myself the death of my husband would be seamless. Our relationship would continue, and we, together, would write this book about terminal illness,

117

dying, death and beyond, (after he died.) We discussed it. He had agreed. I had been studying Near Death Experiences and After Death Communication since beginning my work with Hospice in 1999. However, in truth, I was clueless.

The experience for me was just as it is for everyone: unique, intimate, unpredictable, and difficult. A redeeming grace I found from all the affirmations I had stored in my memory, the list of *expectable reactions to grief*, which I could pull out at appropriate times for comfort. I reminded myself, *anger, tears, confusion, and depression are normal*. I reminded myself, "I too, was not going crazy."

The years between Pancho's diagnosis and death were nothing more than a blur. The truth was, at the end of his journey of cancer, I had no idea how many years it had been since his first diagnosis. I asked myself, "Was it 2002, 2003?" I could not remember. With his diagnosis, I had begun a marathon of coping in my own personal style: rushing, staying busy, and avoiding the pain of the reality to the best of my ability. This is an ill-advised way to cope and one I would never recommend.

My advice to grieving clients would have been to experience the pain of grief as they encountered it, to be honest with themselves and sit with the pain. However, part of the uniqueness of the grief experience is what we bring to grief: our personalities, our previous experience with death, our spiritual beliefs and the relationship that was ending.

My personality type on my favorite indicators of personality types, the Enneagram, was a seven. I would defensively remind people when they looked at me with a jaundiced eye, "The way 7's cope under stress is to avoid emotional pain, to stay busy in a flurry of activity." That is exactly what I did. I was too educated in this whole process. I was so educated I would utilize my own advice and 'medicine' to cope. You know what they say about people who try to be their own doctors. I made all the mistakes blindly, in the manner people do when they are under stress.

Chapter Twenty-Eight
Re-Entry

I returned home from the 3-month grief quest in July, leaving Melissa to complete the El Camino on her own. I went back to London and spent several more nights near the White Eagle Lodge. I was there at a moment of history. The London Lodge was moving. Along with a committee of members, I attended a workshop intended to bridge the gap of change the London Lodge was undergoing. They were selling the property on Kensington High Street. Colum rented a space he hoped would draw more young people. He wanted to keep the White Eagle / Cathar message of love alive and vital in today's world.

There are so many stories I could share but this is a travel log of my grief so I have kept the story brief. Colum kindly drove me to the airport and I brought home a case of *Cathar View* books, which I hoped to help promote in America. I was not sure how I would handle being home but I had to try and I was excited to hold Finn, my new grandson!

I used frequent flyer miles to book a roundtrip ticket to take me home from London and give me a flight back in October. I planned to use the return ticket to bring Melissa home from Norway on a repositioning cruise, this time crossing east to west and porting in Fort Lauderdale. My lofty goals for writing 'our' book about death were diminished when I lost the 18 pages I had written in a computer crash. I did not pick the writing up again until February of 2014.

So I was flying home again. While I was in Europe, Butch was taking care of my property. He had turned the yard into a garden, a welcomed surprise. Of course, I could not wait to get my hands on Finn! That was our first stop before anything. Lissa, Beth, and mother drove straight to Treve and Page's house. I came home to a completely new role. I was a widow and I was a Grandmother. I now understood all I had heard from the grandmothers in my life. Treve and Page were adoring parents. Page was nursing Finn and Treve already had his son's life planned as a professional surfer. Treve carried Finn around on his shoulders from the time he was tiny. Finn was blessed in that both his parents were able to share in his care.

Unfortunately, at home I went into a funk. I do not remember much about the summer months. I struggled to get out of bed and accomplish anything. I did not feel like working, writing, cleaning, organizing. Finn was the only light I could find. Repeatedly, I felt myself wandering in circles. Lissa and Beth returned to being my early morning support team as I continued to mourn. I kept expecting more of myself but was not able to find it. I continued to audio journaling. Thinking back, I could remember little between July and October. October was when I used my return ticket back to Europe to meet Melissa.

November was the first anniversary of Pancho's death. I invited Melissa to come home with me on the repositioning cruise. I was able to use the other half of my ticket that I had booked in the summer in order to fly back to London in late October. Melissa asked me to come to Norway and stay for a few days before we flew back to London to catch the ship. Melissa's cute friend, Alex, whom she met in Croatia picked us up at the airport and entertained us to a point of "laughter tears" that evening. We spent the night with his Grandmother, not far from the port, and Alex dropped us off at the cruise ship just prior to its leaving.

The cruise home with Melissa was much nicer than the cruise over in April. It was even fun. Elizabeth Palin and her daughter, Denise, joined us. Melissa appointed herself as my life coach and started to work on me. We climbed the eleven flights of stairs, did yoga and workouts almost every day, ate spectacular/healthy meals, and even went Disco dancing one night. We were in the middle of the Atlantic on November 6, the first anniversary of Pancho's death.

I still had one of the small flat round stones I had found on the beach at Nerja, Spain, which I had transformed into markers to be left along the Camino. I had written Pancho on each one and Melissa had carefully left them on the trail. At the place where we parted, Melissa going on to Santiago and I going back to Biarritz to return home, I buried the walking stick in the ground like a spear. On it, I had carved Pancho's name. It was at Cruz de Malpica where there is a cross high upon its hill. Someone had painted Buen Camino on the bridge and I took a picture. "Buen Camino, Pancho." I whispered. I cried all the way back to the car. I left Melissa to her much needed solitary grief in Spain.

At sea, on the anniversary of Pancho's death, Melissa and I stood on the deck looking out at the setting son. We used the little stones, some flowers, and a small jade beetle and ceremonially cast them into the water remembering Pancho. Throwing them in, I imagined them floating down, down, down, and landing on the bottom of the ocean. With our right hands, we formed the shape of a heart and took a picture. Back in the cabin, I took a picture of the television screen that indicated on a map the spot showing our position in the Atlantic. Pancho loved the ocean so much.

Pancho was quick to send us signs following the ceremony. The night of the anniversary of his death, nestled in our cozy dark cabin, we both awoke at the same time. It was pitch black in the room but as the time changed an hour every other night as we traveled back through time zones, we never knew what time it was. Melissa asked me to hand her a Tylenol and check the time. I pushed the button on the top of my phone to turn on the screen. It was 6:22, June 22, Pancho's birth date. It was the reoccurring sign. We were both amazed. Next, he sent me a rose.

Pancho actually sent roses in a variety of ways. "I want Dad to send me a rose," I told Melissa. She kept saying, "You can't do that!" "Why not?" I asked, "I always ask him for signs and I want to know he hears us! Melissa pointed out the first rose. It was in a painting we passed everyday on the stairs, "There's your rose Mom."

Returning to our cabin, a steward walked right in front of us carrying a red rose. I almost stopped her but Melissa held my arm. We got on the elevator to see someone holding a red rose. Finally, we went to a Karaoke talent show. As we walked into the theatre, I reached down on the floor and picked up a rose at my feet, one I could keep. It was an artificial red rose. I was satisfied but Pancho was not through. One of the contestants named Rose had chosen her song, "The Rose." As she sang, Melissa whispered, "I love that song." Then Melissa turned to me, with a wide-eyed stare, "THE ROSE!"

Chapter Twenty-Nine
Après Anniversary

Returning from the anniversary cruise with Melissa, I attempted to settle back in at home, <u>again</u>! It was still hard to face. Two weeks after we got back I went into the hospital for a full knee replacement and as a result, I moved downstairs into the living room in front of the fireplace on a couch that made into a futon bed. Sleeping in a different location made home easier.

Melissa came home with a determination to help me get through my grief. She wanted to clear away the past, including Pancho's clothes and "things." We had accumulated all the 'stuff' left over from Pancho running a 20-year business on our property: trailers, boats, motors, clam bags, stakes, counting tables, and crab traps. Pancho's domain had remained untouched and waiting.

Melissa approached it like a superhero. Having been a nomad for a couple of years, she had no home and converted my current home office back into her bedroom, the one from her youth. She faced my lifetime of "things" with a passion and a mission to help me clean the slate. I realized between my physical recovery from surgery and facing the holidays I had encountered the next stage of grief, depression. I, who had always been energetic, the action taker, was now willing to step back and let her take the lead. I gave her permission to make the changes to the house she envisioned and she set about advertising all of the vehicles. We not only had boats and trailers, we had Pancho's pop-up camper and a Coachman RV. The amount of "stuff" had overwhelmed Melissa and me as well.

We made it through Christmas. I do not remember much. I had a right to be depressed, I told myself. I had just gotten through the anniversary of Pancho's death and Thanksgiving Dinner (which Melissa had cooked). I attempted to avoid Christmas. Unlike the previous year, when I had flown to Mexico and spent Christmas day on the plane, I tried to avoid the holidays from my living room couch with ice packs and my knee propped high while I recovered from the surgery.

Melissa bought a tiny blue spruce and we put it by the fireplace in my makeshift bedroom. I hobbled around. Physical therapists visited my house. I did not go Christmas shopping. My gifts came from the grocery store where I bought gift certificates.

My one-year-old grandbaby Finn made everything seem better. Being a grandmother, rocking and holding him, took my full focus and heart. He helped me heal, as I know he did Melissa. By February, we both needed a snow break. Melissa flew off to California to go skiing with her good friends at Mammoth Mountain.

I was home alone for the first time. Debbie, a friend for almost 40 years who I met even before I met Pancho, was home for her birthday. We went out to dinner and both of us got sick the next day with flu. I was sitting in bed and entertaining my depressed thoughts. I just could not snap out of it. It felt like I was walking through mud and I reminded myself depression comes before reconciliation when grieving. It was unavoidable; it was inevitable.

I was in bed having a hard time getting up when I pulled my laptop onto my lap and started reading my email. I received a notice from my airline miles. Upon opening it, I saw I had over 50,000 miles. That was enough to get to Montana. I knew because that was what I had been saving them for. Fred and Debbie had invited me to come any time, so I called Debbie, "Why don't I go home with you, I'd love to see some snow."

She thought it was a crazy idea with us both sick but welcomed my company. We were able to get on the same plane. I got my wish, the snow was 6 inches deep when we arrived and kept falling, creating over a foot on top of the picnic table in their backyard and laying thick white blankets on all the branches of the pines.

The trip was a salve to my aching soul, as was spending time with Debbie, Fred and their horses. Because I did not have to go out in the snow, unless I wanted, I felt like I was living inside a postcard with a different beautiful view from every corner of the house.

In the evenings, a full moon rose over the horses nibbling their hay in the backyard. One afternoon we saw a beautiful rainbow. Thanks, Pancho. Debbie and I talked about Pancho, and I for the first time since his death felt like I could write. That was when I began this project once again.

Chapter Thirty
Valentine's Day 2014

*When someone you love dies, you naturally question
the meaning and purpose of life. You may doubt your
faith and have spiritual conflicts and questions racing
through your head and heart.*
Journey through Grief,
By Alan Wolfelt

Alan Wolfelt nailed it when he described the journey
through grief. I had read his article to grief groups so
often that it was almost committed to memory. That
did help when grief came into my own life. The
hardest part was that I had had the illusion my
spiritual beliefs would sustain me. I was not angry
with God anymore; I was left with only doubts. Did I
believe all of those things I thought I believed or was
I, as I told my clients, *brought back to my knees,
questioning everything?*

That is the reason I was so demanding of Pancho. I
wanted him to give me proof, and even though I had
received numerous signs, they were not proof
enough. Snow-bound in Montana, I was left in a quiet
house while Debbie and Fred worked. I was alone
with views of the picturesque horses, long fences and
mountains in the backdrop, and white snow covering
everything. I decided I needed to re-read my own
work, *The Magdalene Awakening*. I pulled Debbie's

copy off the bookshelf. I knew it was an affirmation of all the spiritual beliefs I had come to in my lifetime, up to the moment of loss. The reading helped.

The Magdalene Awakening reminded me of my beliefs. I had forgotten the lessons I had taught so many people. It does not matter how much you know, grief comes to walk beside you when death touches your life and there is NO WAY to escape the pain, regardless of your knowledge. I was no different. Grief is *the stuff* of the heart, mine being a broken heart. I remember thinking, "Now, I know what that expression means, because it literally feels like there is a broken cavity in your chest, emptiness and physical pain."

Re-reading, *The Magdalene Awakening,* brought tears to my eyes when I read the final passage in the book: "Death…is the final initiation. When death stands with arms held open and we can no longer put him off, we welcome him as a friend. A gentle friend who guides us on to a world that is beyond this ego world. For death is a win/win, another incredible journey…" and now, I will add "to the greatest mystery."

When I finished reading my book, I wondered why I could not write. I was miserable not writing. What kept me from writing? I was in a cocoon. I needed to put wood on the fire of my life literally and symbolically. The open fireplace at Debbie's house brought me comfort but my own fireplace lay cold the year after Pancho died. I had burned all the wood he had left stacked on a woodpile during the first winter after he died.

The second winter found me trying to find new sources to fuel the fireplace. The cold hearth at home left me chilled and immobile, directionless. I could be doing so much with my time since I had retired. I had so few real responsibilities but it felt like I was stuck in cement. I could do nothing. I felt the frozen chill of the empty hearth.

Alone inside Debbie's house on Valentine's Day, still dealing with the sniffling from the flu, I started to write. Outside the snow had begun to melt and along with the thaw outside, there seem to begin a thaw inside. Since it had snowed more that winter than in 30 years, the melt caused a flood in the barn, meaning Debbie and Fred were busy outside with tractors and trying various schemes to figure out how to save the hay that was scarce at this time of the year. I tried to help move a few bails but eventually I returned to the house, built a fire and decided to watch a sappy Valentine's movie alone.

It was a World War II story, a modern movie with Betty White playing the wife of a soldier who had gone missing in action over 66 years before. They had parted for the last time on Valentine's Day, he waved from the train and went off to war. He went missing in action, and his death was never confirmed. Every year she would go to the stations on Valentine's Day still waiting. A young woman reporter, decided to write feature on her story. The reporter was able to creatively investigate and find out what happened to her husband. She found out where he was buried in the Philippians. After 66 years, his body was returned home on the train....on Valentine's Day.

That day would have been our 40th Valentine's Day together. I thought back on a special ring Pancho had given me for our first. I had put it in the safety deposit box along with all my jewelry not feeling like wearing any while I grieved.

In the Valentines Day's movie, Betty White's character stopped her grandson from digging up a dead rose bush in her front yard because her husband had planted it not long after they were married. "Just cut it back and it might come back," she told him. When she returned home from the train station on that Valentine's Day, there was a single red rose bud on his bush.

When I saw the rose bud on the screen, I rather gasped. I jumped up to take a picture of the television. A red rose bud, and it looked almost exactly like a picture I had taken only a few days before I left Florida of a single rose bud on the rosebush Pancho had bought for his mother's memorial. I, too, had thought the bush was dead and had been delighted to see the single rose.

I took a picture and sent it to Melissa. A red rose bud from Pancho for Valentine's Day. I recognized we had started to develop a different form of a "continuing relationship." Therefore, on Valentine's Day, 2014, I nestled down into the cozy covers and snuggled up with Debbie's feather pillows and I wondered, "Could it be that I will never see you again, Pancho?" It was still so hard to believe.

That night I had a dream of Pancho. It made me look at the fact that the experience I had hoped would be so seamless, real and vivid, was just as Alan Wolfelt

131

described it. It was different, too different for my taste. There had not been a single day, maybe not even a single hour when I had not thought about Pancho. Pancho was still very much a part of my life. However, the signs he brought, the roses, the rainbows, his name "Poncho", stamped upon the price tag of a sweater I pulled off the rack while shopping with Debbie in Missoula's quaint downtown district, were the only relationship we could have. I remembered a quote I had used in the foreword of *The Magdalene Awakening*. It was from one gospel found among the Dead Sea Scrolls, the gospel of Phillip. Mary Magdalene answered the questions from the disciples when they wanted to understand how she had communicated with Jesus outside the tomb. Mary instructed, "It's our shared 'mind' that's in-between us. He does not see through the soul nor through the spirit, but with 'mind' that is between the two, 'mind' is what sees the vision..." Is that what Pancho and I had? Was our new relationship 'our shared mind?'

At Debbie and Fred's house, I had warmed the rooms by stoking the fire, the fire in their hearth, the fire in my heart. I took a picture of a rainbow over her horses in the snow, a rainbow from Pancho. When I arrived home, I aspired to go back to the top of one of my lists, Peru. I was busy making plans for Brazil and Peru when I heard a brisk knock at the door. Pancho was gently rapping again.

Erin, my niece, now living across the street in the shared family house of her grandparents, burst in with her youngest, Avery, in her arms. "I just saw a deer swim the river and get up on our property!" "It had to be a sign from Uncle Pancho," Erin exclaimed, full of adrenaline, "I know it's a sign. I feel like I've been

132

saved by Jesus!" Only someone who has had that experience could understand the elation she felt. "Uncle Pancho told me he'd seen a deer swim the river and I just saw it with my own eyes!"

I, myself, had been on the property for many of my 61 years and never had I seen a deer swim the river. Pancho kept an assortment of binoculars to watch the deer. He had been a hunter all his life, but after receiving the cancer diagnosis, he generally just watched and photographed from the tree stand. It had to be a sign from Pancho and it certainly was a sign for Erin.

Chapter Thirty-One
Traveling with Pancho

On Marriage: "You were born together, and together
you shall be for evermore. You shall be together
when the white wings of death scatter your
days. Aye, you shall be together even in the silent
memory of God."
The Prophet by Khalil Gibran

Whether in the front seat of the truck putting miles on
the tires or flying over vast expanses of water, Pancho
and I were always happy traveling together. I carried
a notebook and would make a list of other places we
wanted to go while we planned our future. Peru was
at the top of our list, but that entry was never
scratched off.

Pancho introduced the world to me after we met. I
had already traveled a good bit because of my
grandmother's home in Nova Scotia. I have driven
the east coast of the United States numerous times and
flown a few times.

By age 22, Pancho had been to many places. When
he graduated from high school, he left for the islands
to work on sailboats. He spent time on all the
Caribbean islands. He worked on one sailboat that
was being delivered to San Diego from St. Croix
through the Panama Canal.

That trip took him up the coast of Mexico where he had visited Zihuatanejo. I always remember his tales of that journey because at that port a woman had begged him to take her daughter with them on the boat to escape their poverty. The captain, who he called Captain Merida, would not let him, good thing! As soon as Pancho's feet hit land in San Diego, he left for the airport to catch a plane home. His travels continued to surf spots in Puerto Rico where he lived in Rincon for a while and to Columbia in South America.

When we met, we took a trip to Puerto Rico, St. Thomas and Jamaica. It was the spring after I graduated from college. We met during my last semester at the University of North Florida where I was getting a degree in psychology. Then we drove together to Nova Scotia for the first time to be followed by many other returns over the years.

He took me to England, France, and Spain for my first time. He proposed in Nice. We stayed for a while in Gibraltar and took a hydrofoil to Morocco. Once we crossed over the border and drove into the Italian Alps. When the kids were young, we went to 23 states in 24 days pulling a camper. We continued to camp with the children as they were growing up.

We just loved to travel. In our later years, almost all the trips we made together had a surfing theme. We went to Costa Rica and on our 25th wedding anniversary Pancho got to surf in Hawaii. We went to Panama and as I mentioned earlier Pancho even carried a surfboard with us on our last trip to Spain and France. I have a picture of Pancho on the shore of Biarritz watching the surf, the same place I would reconnect with Melissa after his death. However, together we had never been to South America and Peru was always a goal. Neither had we been to Brazil where John of God, the healer from Abadiania who had been healing people for the last 35 years does his work. After Pancho received the long distance healing sent from John of God, he said he had tasted "Brazilian Wood" as I mentioned earlier. Pancho felt it was significant, a sign of help and healing. He experienced it several times.

The trip to South America I made with Melissa in May of 2014 had come unexpectedly. Melissa and I would soon find ourselves surrounded, completely engulfed by Brazilian wood, in a home owned by an architect on Boipeba, an island off the coast of Salvador in Brazil. The open walls, the floors, the showers, the bed, the walkway were all made from the dark wood of Brazil. How did I get to Brazil? It was the culmination of Melissa's action plan to pull me out of the dumps and get us traveling. I rather drug my feet and said, "Well, if you can pull it off, I'll go."

Returning home with Melissa from Norway on the cruise commemorating the first anniversary of Pancho's death, and surviving the holidays for the second year had been hard. I listened to my journal and "depression" was the key word, but the trip to Montana with Debbie had lifted my spirits greatly!

Debbie was not used to seeing me so down and she did not want me to write or talk about Pancho because she thought it made me sadder, but I had begun to write again. The writing flowed and it felt great. I had hopes of finishing the book about Pancho in Brazil. During the time leading up to my flight to Rio

136

de Janeiro where I would meet Melissa and her traveling companion, Jenny, I stayed very busy.

From doing nothing, I soon found myself back into a flurry of activity. My 94-year-old mother had been displaced by the DOT, imminent domain had taken her home of 40 years to expand a highway in Jacksonville. My sister had to find a house and relocate our mother. During the first weeks of April, I stayed with my mother. I was working for a company that provided crisis intervention during that same period. Between those two things, I was kept busy.

The process of getting a Brazilian visa was no small task. I waited until the last minute starting in mid-February, but I had to get a yellow fever shot and provide a wide variety of financial information and an itinerary, which I did not have. I also had to send, along with the application, my passport to the Brazilian Embassy in Miami. I accomplished the task exactly 30 days from the date of my departure.

I became concerned when I had heard nothing only days before I was to leave. In the meantime, Jenny, Melissa's friend and travel mate for South American, had talked her Aunt Barbara into flying to Rio for 9 days and Barbara and I started to text and email each other.

Barbara found out that she could get her visa in 10 days if she went into the Embassy and returned to Miami to pick it up. The day we were to fly out was the day her visa would be waiting for her. We encountered numerous obstacles to our trip. It came down to the very last moment. Our flight was booked to leave Miami at 6:30 PM on Monday April 28,

2014. The mail came the day before, but the mailbox was empty.

I was nervous, setting up alternative plans, but I was determined to give it every shot. Typically, I was living by the seat of my pants. The embassy was not taking phone calls. They made it clear that if the application was mailed in, the application had to be returned by mail.

The Embassy had my passport! I could not even go to Peru, which did not require a visa. I had decided to go to Peru in honor of Pancho, hoping once again to find a finish line to my emotional roller coaster so I could move on and begin to start making plans for my future instead of clearing up the past. My ticket was non-refundable.

Again, I asked Butch, who knew Miami well, if he would watch my house as he had done the previous spring and drive us to the Miami airport. He agreed. We arranged to meet Barbara off the Florida Turnpike near Orlando. I drove from Palm Coast to Ocala to pick up Butch and we met Barbara around 11:30 AM.

The rest of the day we drove, and found a room at the Marriott not too far from the embassy and the airport. I told them I wanted to be there when the Embassy opened so I could at least ask what was going on with my passport and pray that by some miracle I would get my visa and make the plane by 6:30 PM.

The embassy opened in the morning only for people making applications. Butch drove us and planted himself in a restaurant with our car in the parking lot. Barbara and I went in, we got a number, and waited, and waited, and waited. I had faxed a letter explaining my predicament and had a copy of that fax along with all my other pertinent information with me.

Michelle, the only worker behind the counter, finally called my number, and I went up. "I'm sorry.," she said, "There is a long line and I cannot stop to check and see if it is still in the office now. If you come back at 3:00 PM when your friend picks her visa, I will have time to look." At least we had some hope. Barbara was not used to the ease with which Butch and I trusted our angels to intercede on our behalf.

Frankly, Barbara thought we were nuts. She had heard a woman flatly turned away the day she put in her application because of the rule about mailing but did not tell me until later. She told her friend Becky, "I hate to say this but there is no way she is going to get her visa today."

Still, I held out hope. I prayed to God and every angel on my list. We even stood in a circle in the room at the Marriott and joined in prayer, asking God's will be done, knowing that is all there is.

We left the Embassy and went back to the hotel. Barbara and I did a little shopping for something warm in case the "winter" weather in Brazil required it and Butch waited at the hotel. We picked him up at 2:00 PM and arrived at the Embassy at 2:30 PM. Again, we took a number. This entire time we were getting frantic text messages from the girls. They wanted to know if we were going to make the plane.

The girls, Melissa and Jenny, had been backpacking all over South America and were waiting for us to arrive to enjoy a little luxury. Again, we had to wait, this time my heart was pounding in my ears. I saw a sign from Pancho on the television screen. A little green parrot was portrayed as the newscaster's helper and that gave me hope. Only I would notice something like that and take it as a sign! I imagined Archangel Michael, tall and grand with his wings wrapped around us. It was 3:00 PM and the windows did not open. It was 3:11 PM and finally the shade was pulled up. Several people, including a pregnant woman, skipped ahead without a number. The embassy attendants were calm and patient.

I started to get more nervous, in fact, I was a wreck. We had the second and the third number. Barbara's number was called and they handed her visa. I was next. It was not the same girl! "Where's Michelle?" we asked, "She had all my documentation." I did not have the application number; it was all on the paperwork given to Michelle. We panicked. She looked at me as if I was crazy. Our plane leaves at 6:30 PM. My passport is either here or in the mail. I begged her for help.

She asked me to write down my name and birthday. It seemed like forever until she returned. However, when she did she had a large white envelop in her hand. She passed it through the window. "Is this it?" I asked. "Open it and make sure," she said now smiling at me. I opened the package. There it was my passport AND my visa.

Barbara started screaming with joy in a room that was dead quiet. She bounced toward the door and kissed the guard whose eyes grew wide as we turned the corner. "We're going to Brazil!" she yelled to everyone in the hall and on the elevator. "Stay calm, Barbara," I said, "We still have to make the plane. It's Miami, let's keep moving."

In addition, it was not just Miami traffic at 3:20 PM. There was a wreck on the highway. I was sticking my head out the window begging the drivers to let us over and they complied. We made it to the airport and finally found the right terminal, jumped out of the car, grabbed our bags, and Butch called out, "I'm not even going to get a kiss?" "Oh," I looked back. Quickly we turned around and kissed him on the cheek then got in line to check our luggage. We were going to Brazil. It truly was a miracle.

Chapter Thirty-two
Rio to Boipeba

We flew all night, changing planes in Bogotá and arriving in Rio at 6:00 AM. The girls had rented a car, such a daring pair, and were there to meet us. It took a little while to find us, but we had made it! Melissa had done another home exchange with a couple in Rio, good girl! She had a contact who was a friend's cousin, Claudio, who lived there.

Claudio became our guide and companion. With Melissa and Jenny, two gorgeous girls in tow, I am sure he did not mind. We did every tourist "thing" you could do in Rio; the Botanical gardens, Ipanema Beach, Copacabana, Sugar Loaf, which is a lift taking you to the top of the city with spectacular views. We ate, drank, and the girls and Barbara went hang gliding, paddle boarding, and surfing.

In the mornings, we did Yoga on the private beach below our condominium. The building was four stories, each condominium had a full wall-sized window overlooking the ocean. The kitchen was equipped with a juicer so we juiced and ate healthy meals. A tourist's dream, but there was something else I had hoped we could do.

It was after I bought my ticket and sent for my visa I was lying in bed I realized, I am going to Brazil, John of God's Brazil! Maybe I could go see John of

God. I sent an email off to Carol Pessin, the friend who had been in Brazil when we had appealed for healing from John of God. She sent back a half dozen links to everything I would need to know if I wanted to go to the Casa. I wanted the others to read about John of God and I pulled it up on the computer. However, I kept hearing this annoying sound, like the call of a bird. I handed the computer to Melissa so she could read about John of God. "What is that? Is that a cat?" Melissa asked. "No," I wondered, just recognizing the sound. "It's a Parrot!" I exclaimed and looked out the window and there on the balcony was a GREEN Parrot. "Pancho! Perhap we are supposed to go!" I called out.

I had the others convinced. Melissa found a reasonable flight but it left in about 45 minutes. We would have to leave now! Instead of booking tickets, we decided to drive to the airport and try from there. Within 10 minutes, we were in the car, in traffic, trying to make it to the airport. We pulled in with only minutes before the flight took off. Melissa waited outside and we checked every airline. It was too late and too expensive. *All is in divine order. I did my best*, I told myself, *if I were supposed to get there, John of God would get me there.* We ended up being close to Sugar Loaf and went on to have an extraordinary day and evening with dinner at the foot of the mountain.

Each day seemed better than the day before as four travel mates enjoyed Rio together. Melissa drove like a champion through the crazy traffic. We met nice people. The girls went out to the multi-level dance bars to try Salsa dancing. We watched young men play soccer on a court near our condominium and on the beach. *Could there be anything better?* We asked. In addition, that is what I thought too, until we arrived by skiff on the island of Boipeba.

I realized that once again I attempted to avoid my sadness through movement and travel. I still felt so lost whenever I sat still. Every morning I awoke to remember Pancho was gone and life continued to feel empty. At least when I was in a new bed, in a different place, I woke and had to remind myself where I was. My style of grief coping was a luxury most people cannot afford but I had already figured out how to include travel and adventure in my life. I knew myself and I knew travel and adventure correlated with happiness. Melissa had been clever and done home exchanges, traveled with backpack and on buses and had made the trip affordable for both of us.

The first property Melissa found to exchange was on Boipeba Island off the coast of Brazil south of Salvador on Bahia. "No cars," she said, "only horses for transportation."
"Sounds good to me." I replied.
"We can write our book." she added.
"Sounds great to me!" I delightedly concluded.

On May 6, we ended our stay in Rio. We all converged at the airport and went in different directions. Jenny and Barbara flew home. Melissa and I went on to a hotel we had booked in Salvador on the way to Boipeba. The manager, Jullianno, was dubious about our plans. Why would you want to go there? It is a dangerous trip.

Safety had been my concern as well when Melissa first suggested traveling in South America. She was determined to visit every continent while she had freedom. I had heard so many scary things about South America but I could not have been more wrong. The people we met were kind and gentle.

The locals did think we were a bit too trusting. You find that attitude in America, too. There are only two choices really, love or fear. After my long experience with *A Course in Miracles*, I chose to trust. Melissa had learned the same. She told me a story about a young woman who was hired to work along side her on a yacht. The girl was offered the job because one of the crewmembers had called her over to chat and asked her if she was looking for work. The girl said to Melissa, "I was afraid at first. My mother told me I should not trust strangers." "Really?" Melissa puzzled, "My mother taught me there aren't any."

Jullianno was Italian; his wife was Brazilian. She assured him it was a beautiful place to visit. Jullianno with broken English helped us map out a plan. He drew out the route we would have to take. First, we had to take a taxi, then a catamaran, then a bus or taxi, and then a boat to the island. "We can do this," we assured him.

After breakfast, our cab arrived and we headed for our first stop, the port. The cab ride took a little less than an hour and cost a little less than 100 Reals (2.22 Reals to the dollar, at that time). The catamaran was less than 8 dollars and it took us to the next point where we were going to check on prices for bus and cab. Jullianno told us it might be dangerous to be traveling on a bus, "Someone might rob you with a gun." However, we continued to have faith in humanity, so much so, we accepted a ride in a shared van to Valencia.

It was a ratty looking white van but the older woman in the front sear assured us it was safe. The driver quoted us 30 Reals each. We looked at each other, shrugged our shoulders and climbed in. Another man joined the crowded front seat and we were off. We drove over dusty roads full of construction ruts and bumps, but our driver did not slow down, no sir. He was getting up there in an hour and a half as he promised. He offered us a banana from a bundle in the back and we graciously accepted.

We even got a bathroom break at the gas station. Only a few times we thought, well they could hold us for ransom, steal our money, and murder us, rape! However, I just let those thoughts flow on through, and our driver delivered us right to the port to catch the skiff. No one spoke English and some spoke Spanish. People speak Portuguese in Brazil!

We used every language in our repertoire, mine mostly French, and a little Spanish. Melissa did very well. We waited for the skiff and after an hour's ride pulled up to the colorful port of Boipeba. Melissa ran off to find a bathroom and I stood watch over our bags. Melissa had been traveling with her hiker's backpack. I had my small carry on and a backpack but mine was not conducive for pulling in the sand. We had been assured it was only about an eight-minute walk. I thought the kids with the wheelbarrows looked very tempting but Melissa was sure we could do it ourselves.

She fussed at me the entire time for not being an efficient packer, but helped most of the way dragging my bag and her packs. At the last minute, we were rescued by Viktor, the caretaker of the property. He was originally from Madrid. He had arrived on the island as a part of a reality show from Spain. He won, and had chosen to make Boipeba his home.

I had no idea how long and hard the walk was as we climbed the steep paths to arrive at the palatial retreat at the top of the hill overlooking the ocean. Red faced, heaving, with boogers hanging from my nose, we stood with our mouths opened as we took it all in. It was all ours for 15 days. Our flights left Salvador on May 25. As I walked around and looked at our home for the next couple of weeks, I was seized by the memory of Pancho tasting Brazilian Wood. There was Brazilian Wood all around us, and parrots!

Melissa went for a walk and came back quite excited, "You are not going to believe this Mom! I saw two green parrots and they climbed up my arm! One got caught in my hair, it took 10 minutes to get him out!" Pancho!

Oh yeah, I have one more parrot story. A few days into our stay in Rio, I was standing by the glass window looking out over the ocean. I heard a wolf whistle, you guessed it, Pancho, the green parrot. My Pancho was still trying to be funny. I felt certain he had a premonition about our future with Brazilian Wood and we felt his presence everywhere.
After I wrote this, Melissa and I walked down from our perch retreat to the beach to have dinner. She took me to meet the green parrot that had entangled

itself in her hair the day before. He got on my arm and if you could believe this, he puffed up his feathers and wolf whistled, twice! Oh, and by the way, I was reading the history of Boipeba Island and found this: The economy of the Bahian coast was exclusively one of extraction for three centuries. The target was brazil-wood, highly valued by European dye merchants. Perhaps, Pancho was experiencing our future "relationship" when he tasted "Brazilian Wood."

Chapter Thirty-Three
Island Life: White Horses in the Mist and White Cats in my Window

From the mist on the beach, the form of a white horse took shape. It was walking toward me. Kirsti said, "There is your sign." Kirsti was the Dutch beauty minding the restaurant during the dead hours of the rainy season on the Island of Boipeba. We had been discussing signs from Pancho.

"Look, Melissa," I relayed, "Another horse, a white one."

I turned to look over my shoulder to see Melissa, her knees pulled to her chest as she curled in her chair. Her hair was twisted on top of her head to combat the heat. With her phone on her ear, she used the Wi-Fi at the Agua Luar Bar/Restaurant to talk to friends.

I turned back to Kirsti, "That's the second horse that walked up on me on this trip. Yesterday, I was sitting on the beach and I heard something moving behind me. When I turned around, voila', a horse! I easily caught the horse and walked him down to meet Melissa."

That day Melissa had opted to run while I chose to rest on the sand and take a video of a hermit crab dashing in and out of its hole. We had just enjoyed a delicious Bahian Brunch and Caipirinha (Brazilian drink) a few minutes earlier. The restaurant with its offerings had appeared abruptly, just as we emerged from a clump of mangroves on the white sand beaches while we were exploring. Before the meal was over the high tide was tickling our toes. The currents swept the sand away from the plastic table legs creating little gullies and causing the table to lean. We had finished eating just in time and continued walking. That is when I opted to sit and she opted to run. She was delighted when she returned to find me standing with a lead rope and horse in hand. We had just been talking about horseback riding.

The following morning a white cat jumped in my opened window to join me. She explored the realm of the bungalow, every corner, looking for creatures to slap with her paw and taunting the birds which dove past her while she rested on the ledge of the opened top half of the door shrouded only by the blue, sheer curtains.

All this I witnessed from within my cocoon, made up of my mosquito net, which I lifted and tied back at the corners each morning, soggy with humidity from the rain that had tapped on the straw roof throughout the night. By moving the netting, I allowed the little buzzing vampires who had feasted on my body while I slept to escape. I never quite got the mosquito net right, but it softened the view out the open screenless door and windows and as I am from Florida, I am used to mosquitoes.

It was the rainy season. There were only a few tourists on the entire island. For me, Boipeba was heaven. Behind the sounds of the rain, and the chatter of the birds, was the roar of ocean waves. Several times African drums could be heard in the distance playing around the clock. There were chirping insects and birds I had never heard before along with some bird sounds I did recognize, like the "peep-peep" of the hawk.

I knew the sound of the hawk and I knew the message of the hawk, "Rise above, view life from a distance, look broadly about and see the bigger picture." That was exactly what I had been attempting to do. How blessed I had been by what I brought with me. I had brought one book, *The Cathar View* that I wanted to re-explore.

Though I was a contributor, there were many other excellent accounts of the Cathars written by a wide variety of experts included in the compendium and I had been too distracted by my grief when it came out in October, 2012 to appreciate it. I had a hard time reading after Pancho's death. My copy of *The Cathar View* had arrived for Christmas that year and I was so proud to be a part of it.

Pancho would have been proud too if the copy of the book had arrived just a few weeks earlier. My portion of the book had been a comfort to him, and it was in print. During the months leading up to his death it had given us the perspective of the hawk. It allowed us to "rise above" our one small life within the realm of infinity.

The other jewel that was an unexpected treasure was the PDF version of a book written by Molly Worth's brother, George. It had never been published. He called it, *The Lotus and the Rose*. Molly Worth was the woman I had lived with in England while Pancho went to sea in 1982. During that time Treve, our first son was born. Molly described her brother George as odd but George had been an avid student of world religions and the history of humankind. What I found in George, was the equivalent of a history lesson on the Christian religion and some of the scoundrels that perverted the message of Jesus. I reflected back to the times when I was a teenager struggling with confusion when I read the New Testament and then attended the sermons on Sunday. My favorite version of the New Testament was the one that had all the words supposed to be quoting Jesus, written in red. What George had done was create the same thing for me, but for the Koran as well, and the Bhagavad Gita, the Brahmana's and the Upanishads; all of which I was familiar with but I was far from a scholar. Therefore, during those quiet days on Boipeba Island, struggling with my spiritual beliefs, I had the opportunity to take a deeper look at the greatest wisdoms of all the world's religions and found them to be compatible with my beliefs and with the red-lettered teachings of Jesus.

It is hard to describe the ecstasy of rest, the bliss of truly sitting quietly, distracted only by nature, the rain, the sun, the sound of singing birds and breezes moving through the lush, green growth. Every morning the jungle of Boipeba sprouted new flowers, even though we were told it was winter. Melissa said, "The biggest decision we have to make in the day is which hammock to lie in." Boipeba Island is one of the islands off the southern coast of the state of Bahia, Brazil, which is actually on Brazil's northeast corner. It is surrounded by the ocean on one side, and the Inferno River Estuary on the other.

The island is home to a great variety of ecosystems. It got its name from the Tupy Indians and means, "Flat Snake", referring, in reality, to the sea turtle. Boipeba has its dense Atlantic rainforest, salt marshes, sand dunes, mangroves, coconut-palmed beaches and shallow reefs that are easy to get to for snorkeling.

The island was founded by Jesuits in 1537. It is one of the oldest sites in Bahia colonized by the Portuguese. There are four villages found on the island. The only access to Boipeba is by water. Melissa and I had arrived in one of the water taxis from Valencia to the island's village of Velha Boipeba. We visited Santo Antônio Square at its center to see the Church of the Holy Spirit, the historic monument of greatest importance, dating back to the 17th century. It was constructed by the Jesuits around 1610. We walked through areas of poverty and brightly painted houses. Fishing has traditionally been the primary economic activity, although tourism has increased in the last 10 years.

Fish, shrimp, lobster, clams, and a wide variety of crab are all found off Boipeba's coast and served at the restaurants with rice and beans and a variety of Bahian cuisine. Tropical fruits, coconut, denude (the red fruit of the dendê palm), as well as mangoes, cashews and mangaba (a small native pear-tasting fruit), are all grown on the island. There are no cars permitted on the island - all transportation is either on foot or by wagons pulled by mules or by tractor.

This helps to protect the environment and to promote ecologically minded tourism. People travel from one farm or village to another by boat or by using the local trails. During the first three decades of Portuguese colonization, the Bahian coast provided a support system for the route to India. The Portuguese colonization of the country began in 1516. While researching the history of Boipeba I became even more enamored with her, beyond the fact that the economy of the Bahian coast was harvesting natural resources, primarily *Brazilian-Wood*.

Most of our days we lay in one of the many hammocks provided in shelters by our open living areas, sun bathed on the decks, prepared simple meals or dined on delicious cuisine in the local restaurants. We explored the island fearlessly; walking where we could, sometimes wading through small rivers, and crossing logs like balance beams. We spent late afternoons and evenings cantering the beach on horseback and through the hilly terrain.

To get home at night we had to climb a soggy, red clay path, slick from the evening rains. We learned to maneuver around the gullies the rain created as it washed away a once well thought out trail. Sometimes at night, we followed our flashlights in order to find our way home after dark. We were blessed by a clear night the evening of the full red moon that we watched from the top of the highest hill. Again, as with Pancho so many times, I watched the moonrise as the sun set simultaneously. That evening, we were accompanied by other tourists, Paloma and Rodrigo from Madrid, who shared our food. They were exploring the world not unlike Melissa and me, on a tight budget with backpacks. We all agreed, contrary to the fears of our friends and a family, South America was safe to travel.

South America was inhabited by good, hardworking people and we felt perfectly safe to explore. As we dined, Melissa entertained us with her tales of misadventures in Bolivia, Chile, Argentina, Brazil, and Peru; causing laughter around the table. Yes, we were fearless, until, that is, Kirsti told us about the snakes.

Kirsti said a little girl had been bitten three weeks before by a cobra found on the stairs at the shopping Pavilion. "No," we said in horror, "Cobras? On the beach? You must mean in the jungle." "No," Kirsti shook her head, "They come right out on the beach. We once had a monkey in a cage at the restaurant and it was eaten by a snake!"

Hum, we were glad we only had two more days to worry about running into nasty, poisonous creatures on our path. The next few days we walked with great caution. Melissa cried wolf numerous times. With great, gasping inhales, she would jump, scaring me witless and laughing at me. "Not funny!" I would protest.

The night the white horse came out of the mist on the beach we had gone out to dinner with Kirsti and during the meal, the bottom fell out of the sky. We were sprinkled at our table through the natural palm roof. I had gotten used to that in bed the first night it rained. I put a towel above me on the mosquito net. It never stopped raining that night. We found an open market and Melissa and I huddled under an umbrella we bought there after dinner. I pulled my red shawl tightly over my head and we walked in lockstep the long trail back, wading through the new rivers formed in the streets, rushing over cobblestone and clay tracks. As we waded through the ankle deep rivers, we hoped the snakes did not swim. I guess there has to be a flipside of Paradise.

I thought again about the Brazilian Wood. We were surrounded by Brazilian Wood. Had Pancho known this would be a stopping place for Melissa and me to tie up some loose edges of our grief? It was a place where we could write down some of the details. A place to cry and laugh together, to think and consider where life might take us from here as we prepared again to move in opposite directions in the world.

The end of May found us once again at the cross roads of our shared journeys. It was similar to the one where we parted in Spain on the El Camino. Funny enough, we were, in one-way, trading places. Melissa took my California Pack on wheels and I took her backpack. She was going to Paris, the south of France and Norway. I was going to Cusco, and onto Machu Picchu. We would not meet up again for a while back in Florida at my home. I would one more time check in to see how far I'd come. It was always a measuring point, my re-entry to home, would I then know where I was on the grief journey?

Even the Garden of Eden had snakes and I do not know if we drew one to us because we had been so focused on them, or if I longed for the message a snake brings in Native American lore: transition, change, a shedding of skin, transformation.

The night before we left, the temptation of spending our last Reals at shops in the Pavilion Mall was too much for us, so we ventured out. Melissa led with her flash light and I followed behind, both of us vigilant. That is why we saw it. Melissa caught it in the beam of her flashlight. It was striped, either a coral snake or its nonpoisonous friend. I turned my phone flashlight into its camera, amazed we had actually manifested our fears, and took a picture of the painted beauty.

You could not make it out in my picture but Melissa called it, "yellow on red, friend of Fred." Her father had taught her the rhyme to identify a coral snake. "If it's a King Snake, she said, it's not 'peligro' (dangerous)." We had seen our "snake" so we figured we were safe from then on as both of us confessed to fears that we rarely confessed!

It was time to move on, and the next morning we loaded our pack and bags and headed down to the launch where we said goodbye to the quiet paradise and started the daylong trek to Santiago by shared taxi, ferry, and taxi again. This time we chose a five-star resort on the beautiful white sand beaches of Santiago, not far from the airport.

I had glanced at my ticket and mistakenly thought my flight was 9:00AM. I caught a taxi to the airport only to realize I had the whole day before me, so, because Melissa was staying for a late checkout as she flew to Paris at 5:00PM, I decided to go back to the hotel. I stepped outside the terminal and saw the sign I had been looking for and asking for, a rainbow. It followed me all the way back to the hotel and I smiled as I realized I would have one more day with Melissa, this time to lie by the pool.

We did have to part that evening at the airport and I had a long trip with two layovers, Sao Paulo and Lima, but I did not mind. I was going to be at the "top of our list" Peru, Machu Picchu. I was going alone. I had no plans except to check in at the small hotel a friend Lesley owned in Cusco and I had time to decide what my last nine days in South America would consist of. It was a trip for "us" and it was back to the top of our list. My brain had to shift from Portuguese to Spanish, from Reals, to Sols, and a much higher altitude but I did not care. I was going to be in Peru.

Chapter Thirty-Four
Back to the top of the List: Peru

Peru was a bit of a culture shock. I moved from the isolated island life to a crowded city. The crowded Incan cobblestone roads curved in and around the massive churches, tourist hostels, shops, women and girls dressed in Peruvian bright colors leading or holding baby lamas. The street venders swarmed tourist from all sides offering a variety of wares. I arrived in the morning at the Cusco airport at around 10:00 AM. *No not Bom Dia, Buenos Dias,* I had to think. I had been instructed by Lesley to look for someone holding a sign with my name.

Before I could say "no gracias," a man had scooped up my backpacks and carried them outside. I scanned the crowd, no success. I told him to leave me and my bags, and gave him 10 Soles. I waited for my own ride for five more minutes then decided perhaps that I should call to make sure I was in the right place. I turned to my left and addressed a young man standing on the other side of a rail.   I asked *Hablas ingles*? "Yes." He answered in an American accent.

"Do you know the country code for Peru? I want to call my hostel."

"No." he admitted, "Why don't you just try the number?"

"Good idea," I started to punch the number into the phone. He obviously saw his name on a sign, as he started moving. At the same time, I saw my name. I picked up my packs and began to walk.

"Is your name Shannon?" I asked, heaving my pack onto my shoulder.

"No." he replied. "Then that must be me." I said as I moved in the same direction. Benjamin, the young man from Colorado, and I were sharing the same driver. "That's synchronistic," I commented.

Benjamin was having an exciting spiritual opening and he chatted on about his experiences with enthusiasm. I smiled and listened for the entire drive. I looked down at my phone just as he arrived at his hotel. My phone said 11:11. "Are you interested in the master numbers, Benjamin?" I asked. "Oh yes," he said, especially 22, my birthday in June 22, 6/22." "That was my husband's birthday. That is one way he sends me signs, with the number 622. Thanks Benjamin," I said as he climbed out of the car and we both regretted our brief encounter was ending.

A nice welcome to Peru. *Guess you know I am here Pancho.* The driver continued until we reached the plaza of San Blas in Cusco. He grabbed my bags and walked, I followed. He walked up a set of steps, around a corner, then another, and one more until we reached the Gringo, Leslie's mini hotel and hostel. At the door, he rang a bell and we were greeted by an attractive Peruvian woman. She had limited English skills. I gave her my name and she checked me into my home for the next 8 nights. Well, it was at least the place I stored my luggage as I spiraled out to the surrounding sites.

Melissa had mentioned altitude sickness and suggested I take iron but I had not paid attention. I did not realize how high the altitude was in Cusco and I found myself googling symptoms. I started to have a throbbing headache. It lasted through the night and into the next day. I took ibuprofen and Tylenol and chewed the cocoa leaves left in bowls on the table in the common area. They were a local remedy, legal in Peru. I also drank Cocoa tea. However, the next day I stepped into a pharmacy and purchased a local treatment in capsule form. It was going to take a while to adjust. I limited my activity the first day and went to bed early.

I had no plans, no tours lined up, all I knew was I wanted to go to Machu Picchu and I knew I would figure it out. It was much more interesting being led by spirit even if spirit often took me in circles. I was able to see rainbows and meet the people I was supposed to meet. I saw Leslie and her son, Simon. They were the only people I knew in Cusco. When I decided to make the trip to Peru, I contacted via email and made a reservation. The plan for the week began to take shape. The first thing I did was walk around the city. I had goggled 10 best things to do in Cusco and that included the squares, parks, museum and local ruins.

The first day I ventured out, I walked down the steps we had climbed the first day. I knew I could not get lost if I just followed the one street and came back the same way. I would just go straight down and straight back up. The streets were alive with activity, shops, and crowds. There were hordes of people selling local wares, jewelry and art. I was a sucker at first and ended up buying things I really did not need but thought it was a good opportunity to purchase gifts to take home.

The walk back up to our hostel was steep and I found myself breathless several times before I reached the top. A young girl leading an adolescent lama stopped me for a picture and asked only for a donation. I gave her five Sols and took a picture of her red and orange regalia next to her lama in the afternoon sun. By the time I reached the top I was tired, still affected by the altitude sickness. I took a nap and planned to go to the local ruin with a name that sounded like sexy woman, but was actually Sachiwaman.

Sachiwaman was an ancient sprawling ruin, pre Incan according to a newspaper article I read just before I left the room. I took a taxi to the top where the ruin stood. It was just outside of Cusco. I was still having a hard time catching my breath so I took a leisurely walk around the massive ruin. The rocks making up its walls appeared to have been poured into place. They were massive, thousands of pounds, how did they fit so perfectly? *How did this ancient culture accomplish that*? I asked myself.

My plan was to make the 20-minute walk back down to Cusco. That turned out to be a good choice. Going down was easy but I was relieved I had not tried to walk up. I met a group of young people huffing and puffing just before they reached the top. Rounding a corner, I encountered a lama with a dangling lead rope. Its owner dressed in the native Peruvian attire followed. The funny little top hats and the ease with which the woman bundled their children onto their body by tying a colorful shawl fascinated me. Again, I took a picture and gave her a tip. In this way, local women made their living.

I walked down the cobblestones steps. It narrowed into a path as I reached edge of the town. The twinkling lights of Cusco illuminated the mountains on the far side of the city. Asking a fellow walker, I was directed to take a right turn and found my hotel The Gringo by dusk.

The Gringo cost only 20 dollars a night. I had a charming private room decorated in bright contrasting walls and accented by small altars. The bathroom and shower were shared but conveniently down the hall. It was a crossroad for English speaking people from all over the world. I met many interesting young people. Two young doctors from England who recently finished their hospital residency were touring South America. Another doctor around my age from Puerto Rico brought his son and one of his patients with cancer. She came seeking treatment through a shamanic experience. The city was international, full of young people exploring. I felt so lucky to be able to be a part of this world, so different from my own. I loved the spirit of the young people. In addition, I knew travel is the best education. That is why I always encouraged my children to travel.

That night I slept soundly. By morning, my altitude sickness was gone. Planning my strategy for Machu Picchu was high on my priority for the day. Simon, Leslie's son, said I should plan to stay two nights and take the train so by working with a travel agent around the corner, I booked the rail and a hotel in Aqua Caliente the town closest to Machu Picchu.

She told me it would be most economical to share a minivan and gave me directions to the corner where locals waited in order to pile into the shared vehicles. I was learning how the carpooling transportation worked in South America. Anyone who owned a car could stop by a designated corner and pick up riders to share the cost of gas. It seemed a very sane system.

In this case, it was owners of vans who catered to locals. I would have paid five to 10 times that much had I booked transportation in the tour office. It only cost 10 Sols to get to the rail station at Ollantaytambo where I would catch the Inca Rail. That was Tuesday.

Wednesday, I offered to volunteer for a young woman who was building a clinic. Her practice in occupational therapy was for local children with severe disabilities. She was making devices and chairs out of cardboard. The families would help but she bemoaned her difficulty communicating to the parents so that they would understand their children could gain some independence and mobility with the help of her devices. She said she was desperate for money to buy supplies so I donated to her project, feeling guilty about my hedonistic travel. As she was taking a friend from Boston to Machu Picchu on Tuesday, I was going to try to connect with her on Wednesday and go to Machu Picchu on Thursday.

We were not able to connect so I spent the day in the pre-Columbian art museum, ate at the Vegan Restaurant, and walked to find the place to catch the shared van. I had read there was an agency where I could make a reservation for the planetarium. The planetarium was owned and operated by a local family. That sounded fun but it was with some difficulty that I finally found the right location and I learned too late it was closed in the middle of the day.

I walked on to find ride-sharing corner for the next day, returned to the agency and bought a ticket to look at the stars. I had to be back at the square by 5:40 PM to catch the van to the planetarium and thought I walked briskly. I was five minutes late! However, the van had waited for me and I made it to the Planetarium in time for the show to start on schedule.

The explanation was spoken in both English and Spanish. Inside the dome was a lighted illustration of the skies over Cusco. The owner was an astronomer and he taught us how sailors navigated by using the position of the constellations. I saw for the first time the sky as it appears in the southern hemisphere, the Southern Cross, as well as the Incan constellations.

After the inside presentation, we went outside to look through an enormous telescope through which we could see the sparkling jewel stars around the Southern Cross and the thick milky cloud of billions of stars surrounding it. Some of the stars had exploded long ago and we were witnessing only the light that remained moving in our direction.

We could see Saturn with its rings and one of its moons. Shivering, we were offered blankets to wrap around us and warmed with cups of mint tea. When the presentation was over, we huddled back into the minivan to be taken to the main square.

I hurried up the now familiar steps leading to my hostel. It was about a 10-minute walk from the main square. I was by that time frozen and went right to bed. I had to catch the van to the train in Ollantaytambo by 7:30 AM.

I rose early enough to have fruit for breakfast and catch a taxi to the corner. Unlike Brazil, not a lot of people spoke English. When I arrived, I climbed into the large van. An elderly woman got on board and so she would not have to climb into the back I offered her my seat and moved.

I was joined by a Quechuan man who talked to me in his native tongue and I did my best to understand through makeshift sign language. Before we left, a young man sat between us and we began to talk. His name was Lincoln, named after Abraham Lincoln. He was on the way to begin his new job at the hydroelectric plant. He sang the praises of the Catholic priest and the American congregation who had helped him learn English and complete his education. All of the support had enabled him to qualify for his new job. We began to talk about my grief project and we talked about my signs from Pancho.

"I asked my husband to give me a sign today." I told Lincoln. "I want to see his name in writing. This trip is in his honor. That is why I am going to Machu Picchu alone." Just after we finished that conversation, we both saw it at the same time, PANCHO painted in large letters on the side of a building along the road.

It looked like graffiti but a kind of professional graffiti in that there were other names emblazoned on walls along the road in large letters. I did not have time to take a picture. Lincoln got very excited that my request had been honored so rapidly. "Take a picture of it when you are on the way back!" he said, rather astonished by the synchronicity. We exchanged information and parted in Ollantaytambo. After I returned home, he emailed me with a written version of the mystical story he had told me about his grandmother's death and her signs to him.

After a short wait, I caught the train from the beautifully kept station. The garden around the station was planted with Calla Lilies. This train ride through the mountains is considered one of the most beautiful train rides in the world, literally. From the window, you could see the glaciers on top of the mountains as we moved through multiple ecosystems. The Incan trail wound through the landscape and above the river that cut the sacred valley millions of years ago. Cusco was 7,000 feet higher than the area surrounding Machu Picchu.

I arrived to a rather plain room and decided to go out and eat something but I was only eating fruits and vegetables. On my walk the previous day, I had signed up for a ceremony with a shaman from one of the shops in Cusco called The Portal of Light. It was to take place the night I returned. I had been talked into it by a young man named Edwin who spoke not a word of English but, nonetheless, was so convincing that I agreed. I was searching for Pancho within a shamanic journey.

167

Three days prior I was to eat only pure food, nothing processed, no meat, no sugar or salt. So that night, I ordered a salad, called Beth, and took a stroll around Agua Caliente. It was known for its hot springs. As I was trying to find them, I was coaxed into a massage parlor where I received an Incan massage with hot rocks.

Covered in oil, I left and followed the arrows directing me to the hot springs. My bathing suit was under my clothes so I rented a towel and went to the springs where I sat for about 45 minutes before going back to the hotel to sleep. The walk up to the springs was beautiful but the springs were rather uninviting and crowded but I was not going to miss the opportunity.

I rose early the next morning. I had misunderstood my instructions and arrived at the train station with my ticket to Machu Picchu in my hand. I asked the man who said he understood and sold me an expensive train ticket that I thought was taking me to the Sacred Valley. Unfortunately, it took me back via Peru Rail to Ollantaytambo. This time on the slick, expensive train.

I was delighted by the luxurious view and the information I received from the guide sitting with his clients, an American couple across from me. It was indeed a spectacular ride; one I had not been able to appreciate on the rattier old Incan Rail train. I took lovely pictures of the sunrise over the mountains and was quite happy until I got off and recognized the same station I had left the day before. Hum, I guess Pancho wanted me to enjoy the sunrise from the luxury of that train.

I went to the place to catch a minivan and was told, "You cannot get there from here," by the only person I could find who spoke English. He was wrong. I was going to Machu Picchu. I knew I could, but how was I going to rectify this as I had asked two different attendants if the train I was taking would get me to Machu Picchu and they had said "Yes."

"Not today," they said. "No Cusco." "No, not Cusco, Agua Caliente" I insisted. I still had time to get back and go to the site and I was not going to be told otherwise. Finally, Humberto understood and took me to the train counter and explained to the attendant what had happened. They sold me a discounted ticket back because of the misunderstanding.

I caught the train again and after arriving back in Agua Caliente, immediately identified the direction of the bus. I went back to my room. I plugged in my phone so the battery would last for pictures. I left the room at 11:11am and walked across town to find the bus line. After another short wait, I finally climbed on board and rode the 20-minute ride to Machu Picchu.

I ate some lunch and began the climb on the spectacular ruin, stopping every few yards to take pictures. On the train, I had bought a guidebook so I would understand where I was and I made the giant circle of the ruins climbing high above the terraces pausing to enjoy the view.

My plan was to do a prayer and ceremony for Pancho at 2:22 the time of his death. Before I reached the sacred temple area where that was to take place I met up with a young couple from Washington, DC.

They adopted me for a while as we climbed up to the top and walked along a portion of the Incan trail to see the ancient manmade bridge that could be withdrawn in case of attack by enemies. We took pictures of the Lamas wandering around the site, close enough to touch.

Eventually we parted and I went on alone, completed my ceremony and spent a little time talking to Pancho. "*Was it time to go forward?*" I asked. I kept looking for some kind of demarcation line. I had hoped if I made it to Peru I could find the end point I had been seeking. I asked the question and tossed a Nova Scotia rock Pancho had found for me, one side was black *yes* and one side was white *no*.

"Not yet" was the answer I received. There was more grief ahead of me. Quite honestly, I was relieved as tears streamed down my cheeks. I was not ready to let go. I was here now, was he with me, truly? *Could he see, here, taste and smell through my experience?* I wondered. I made my way back to the entrance being generous with my use of the camera, capturing every scene and I made an imprint with the rubber stamp that said Machu Picchu on my real passport before I exited.

It had been a tough day of climbing for my knee but I was very pleased with the result of the surgery. I could climb again! Physically, I felt great. The combination of exercise, yoga, good pure food and lots of rest had been wonderful for my body. However, by the time I caught the bus to Agua Caliente I was exhausted. I climbed into bed after a shower and slept until early morning. Before catching the train back to Ollantaytambo I walked upstairs to the breakfast room to eat.

At breakfast, I was joined by an Australian man named Ion. He was not very talkative but we were the only two in the room so I started a conversation. I noticed his wedding ring and asked where his wife was. "She died in July of 2012. She and I had planned to come together but we never made it further south than Panama." He said. Ion told me his wife had been diagnosed in June and died a month later. It had almost been two years since her death.

"I'm here for the same reason," I said, "We had always planned to come here, too, but my husband died in December, 2012 and I'm making this trip in his honor." We went on talking and he gave me details about her illness and death. They were married in the hospital the day before she died. Theirs had been only a five-year relationship but he obviously loved and missed her.

I shared a little of our story. "Have you dreamt of her?" I asked. "No," he said, "I talk to her but if she starts talking back then I'll have to be committed." "Not so" I said, going into my story of signs. Tears filled his eyes. I told him I would send him a copy of my rough draft and took his card. "I hope she gives you a wonderful sign today." I said, giving him a list of how that might happen and I said goodbye and left for the train back toward Cusco.

On the train, I found myself facing a couple who ran an eco-travel agency in Bolivia. They told me all about the wonders of Bolivia and made it sound very enticing. I asked what I should see on the way back to Cusco and she gave me some ideas.

I decided to hire a taxi and visit two places, Maras where salty springs stream down from the mountains into tiers of pools and pink salt is harvested and Moray, a beautiful area of circles within circles rising up the hillside. When the train stopped, I walked a short distance to hire a cab.

They were willing to take me to both places and back to Cusco for 160 solos and the driver jumped into the pride of his father in law's fleet, a brand new silver minibus. I had the honor of traveling alone in this new vehicle, unheard of in a country where people pack into the smallest of cars and crowd into shared vans. Considering I paid only 10 solos to get from Cusco, it sounded expensive. However, considering the detours and the time it would take to travel to both sites, it was reasonable.

The driver spoke no English and my Spanish was so poor all I could make out was "Como se Yama?" (What is your name?) "Shannon" I said. "What's yours?" I asked.
"Frank" he said, "Frank, Francisco, Pancho."

"Pancho?" I asked, startled and sitting up straight.

"Si" he answered. I tried to explain. "Me esposo's nombre…was Pancho," I indicted he was in heaven. I felt reassured once again by Pancho's signs.

At the salt pools of Maras, we offered a ride to a couple from France who was hitchhiking. That made the ride a little easier as I practiced my French and he

172

interpreted Spanish between Pancho the driver and myself.

Moray was an area where ancient natives had conducted an experiment in agriculture to see at what level particular plants would grow best using their terraced farming techniques. This was the explanation of the guide. The perfectly circular terraces were impressive. We enjoyed the ride together and exchanged cards. I invited them to couch surf at my house if they found themselves in Florida. I made that offer many times during my travels. I watched carefully on the drive back for the "PANCHO" I had seen written on the side of a building during the van ride up. I had learned from the driver that the painted names along the road were political advertisements. I did not see it again and I was disappointed because I wanted to take a picture.

Back in Cusco, I hurried to my room, showered and prepared myself for the shamanic journey I had arranged before I left. It was to take place at night, from 5PM to 7AM. I would stay in a mountain town through the night. *Was I crazy?* I hoped not. I met Edwin at the Portal of Light and he escorted me to the town in the mountains.

We started in a taxi at the Plaza. We were then taken to a spot where people shared rides to Pisac. Pisac is a beautiful village known to attract ex patriot Gringos kids from Australia, New Zealand, and other places around the world. Three adults shared the back seat with me. We were one big squash. There was a woman in the front seat with a child on her lap. I commented, "That would never happen in America."

173

"I know," the young Australian man sitting next to me said, "I saw the story about the singer Britney Spears back home who was caught driving with her baby in her lap. If someone would presume to put a child in their own seat here, they would be told, *What are you doing? Move that child to make room for an adult*!"

In Brazil, on the road from Valencia to Santiago, Melissa and I had seen a little child clinging to her father on the back of a motor cycle. She could not have been more than three and barely holding on as he made the sharp turns. Neither wore a helmet. We were aghast.

We arrived in Pisca and Edwin led me down the street. The beautiful village situated along a river was littered by dog stools, trash, dark men, and fading sunlight. *What an interesting experience*. I told myself. *Sometimes I cannot believe the things I do.* Edwin pounded on the door and it was opened by a young shaman dressed in his regalia. I was all alone with him for the night.

Chapter Thirty-Five
The Shamanic Journey

I had two initiations that week. A glutton for punishment always pushing myself outside the bounds of sanity, I scheduled another ceremony the day before I flew out. What I did not get at Pisca I hoped to find at the Temple of the moon.

From the heavy massive wooden doorway, I was led to a room upstairs. Edwin assured me the shaman spoke English so I would be okay and that he would make sure I was safely home the next morning. The shaman was about my height, wore jeans and a brightly colored poncho and was about the age of my son. Not exactly what I had expected.

He led me to an upper room and I realized I was going to be the only one present. There was an altar full of crystals and candles. The first thing he did was smudge the room. He did that by lighting sage and spreading the smoke around the room using a large condor feather as a fan. Then he told me a little about the ceremony.

With a condor feather, he cleaned my aura (the space around my body) with the smoke as well and then doused me with some sweet smelling alcohol based liquid, which he sprayed from his mouth. I was instructed to rest and think about why I was there and what I wanted to accomplish. I was told to come up with my three magic words, words I could come back to at any time during the ceremony. I chose: peace, trust and bloom.

He described five stages of initiation and release that were a part of the ceremony. First, I was asked to forgive everyone in my family. I was to bring them before me and forgive them one at a time. When that was accomplished, I was to breathe in, breathe out, and prepare to move on. I would pray that I had truly forgiven them with the help of God and thank Him for helping me. Next, I was to do the same with friends and enemies. Again, I would forgive them with the help of God. I was then directed to ask for forgiveness for my all my bad thoughts. I was asked to forgive my spirit, to forgive myself and heal my body. Finally, I was to ask for forgiveness from all my family friends and enemies.

Each was a stage of the ceremony that he would lead me through by singing and drumming (He handed me a nasty tea which I swallowed to prepare for 3 to 7 hours of work). He came in later to check if I was ready to begin.

I saw my mother and dad. I prayed that I had forgiven them and they had forgiven me. Next, I met with my sibling living and dead and the most significant people in my life. I saw my dark self, reflected in those I thought of as enemy and I acknowledged the dark that existed in me. I thought about those to whom I needed to make amends, people I was no longer in contact with. I then said a prayer and let God do the work as I prayed for healing of my body and forgiveness of myself.

176

He sang and chanted, drummed and rattled, a sliver of a new moon and Venus over his shoulder and a shooting star streaking behind him. I stepped back in time to explore the dark corners of my life. I sat very still and my mind worked hard. He rattled, drummed, and chanted the entire time. I purged the dark self I saw and let it come up and out.

I went to the bathroom where there had been a rat earlier in the evening. I told the shaman and he did a ceremony in the bathroom asking him to leave. I was afraid, but he was gone. When I returned, the Shaman asked if I felt the work was complete. I said yes. He took me to a room with a double bed, clean sheets and a blanket embellished by an American eagle.

The condor and the eagle. I had brought my eagle feather, the one Pancho had found for me at the base of a tree on the clam lease. It was a precious symbol of my Native-American great grandfather and his mother, my Lumbee roots. It represented the powers of the north and I had brought it to the condor feather representing the powers of the south. I had gone in all directions inside myself to explore release and let go but I had not done it with Pancho as much as with all the other important people in my life. The work with Pancho lay ahead.

The morning after the ceremony, the young shaman accompanied me back to my hostel via taxi. We walked the last leg to my home at the Gringo. We chatted in a more general way about our life and beliefs. He told me about his training as a shaman and we were both surprised I had shed so few tears. We had expected my grief to be the primary focus of my journey. That work was to follow. I arrived back at the room just after sunrise and rested all day. After showering, I packed all my things. I knew I would be in the ceremony for 10 hours the next day and would be flying out the next morning.

A half dozen others were staying at the hostel taking advantage of the initiation. We climbed into two taxis and I sat in the front. Once again, I asked specifically for a sign from Pancho as we drove up the mountains from the town. The three others were chatting in the back when I saw *it.*

"Please stop!" I asked the taxi driver. I saw it as clear as day. PANCHO painted on the side of a house. This one I captured. My heart lifted and I knew he was with me in Peru and I hoped that in the quiet of my mind he would meet with me that day once more.

I was joined by Vee Jay and Nor, the two young doctors from England, the older doctor from Puerto Rico and his patient and a beautiful Russian girl named Katarina, a student of philosophy, economics and political science at university in England. There were others as well. Our shaman was white, South African, with long blond hair and she had been living and directing this form of journey into the inner world for many years in Peru.

The massive locked doors opened up onto a beautiful garden with cactus and roses. Though it was winter, it was warm and sunny and after gathering in a circle, we took our mats and found a place to be under the sky with our own mind. I immediately was drawn into my grief and a conversation with Pancho and the tears flowed.

Pancho assured me that my eyes were his eyes, my arms were his arms and every time I held Finn, he held him. And to my asking mind which questioned, "Are you still here Pancho?" I would hear his familiar southern drawl, with a tone that indicated his impatience with me and my infernal questioning still. "Yesssss, Darlin, I'm here." To which I said, "You don't have to say it that way," and he replied, "But you don't ever believe me."

I did a lot of crying for Pancho, missing him, seeing him, releasing him, forgiving him, and asking his forgiveness. I took the symbol of the Snake and the Leopard given to me by an artist in the square the previous day from around my neck. Next to it on the shared chain was my Nova Scotia crystal. I hung them by Leslie's condor feather, which decorated the central pole in the garden. I let them stay there and share the dance of the breeze for several hours.

A stone icon of Ganesh, the Hindu elephant god, was my imaginary companion, helping me over some of my obstacles. The bees and the birds hummed to me under the sky and eventually I peeled off a couple of layers of clothes and inhibition as I lay in the garden and allowed my tears to flow. My fellow sojourners were on their own magic blankets and lay in the sun soaking in the cloudless blue Peruvian sky.

I eventually decided to take a walk to the Temple of the moon, which was just outside the gate. Having to leave the soft music of the garden, I reached into my pack, pulled out my iPod and located the chant of Charlie Standing Horse. They took me back as I relived the walk Pancho and I had made to the Bighorn Medicine Wheel.

179

I carried the chants in my backpack and walked around the broad circumference of the rock cluster before I climbed up to the Temple of the Moon. Taking slow measured steps, I stopped often to admire the green fields and horses that raised their head and paused to listen to the echo of the music in the distant mountains. I slowly made my way back around to the path. There I felt the symbolism of the white crystal and the black Mayan icon now hanging on my neck.

I remembered the black and white columns of Jachin and Boaz, which adorned the Temple of Solomon, another symbolic temple of initiation. I was bringing the Lakota to the Quechua, the eagle to the condor in a ceremonial song and symbolic healing. For the first time in my life, I felt it was too sacred to photograph. I sat in the throne seat carved into the rock at the top of the outcropping and listened to the stories of the Temple of the Moon being told to one of the others by a tour guide.

I entered the cave of the Pachamama, the womb of the mother, the initiation chambers of fertility. I sat on the wide flat stone beneath a portal that allowed the moon light to pour through during ceremony to identify the queen. I allowed my imagination to produce a slide show of all that had taken place over the thousands of years the cave had been honored.

I reconnected with the group and we all walked back together as the ceremony came to an end. We gathered in a circle overlooking the sunset. The sharp cold of the evening called us to pull the layers of clothing and blankets back around our bodies. There we shared our experiences. I showed Lesley the picture of Pancho's sign painted on the house and she knowingly smiled. The taxi came and took us back. Just like every other initiation there were no dramatic messages I took away but a purging had taken place along with some rumblings of change. This I brought home with me the next day when I flew out.

It was time to go home once again

Chapter Thirty-Six
Home Coming and a Wedding

After 20 months, I found myself reviewing, looking back, and sorting almost like sticking my head out of a battered house after a hurricane. I could see the devastation on my life. I was shocked that so much time has passed and that I have been burrowed into my style of coping, cutting myself off from most of the people in my life and moving nonstop. I still have not been still for a long period. At 20 months, I realized I did not remember the last time I cried. The timing of Pancho ashes finally arriving helped fill the emptiness in my chest.

This time I returned from my trip to a wedding. It was countdown to wedding day for my son Treve and his fiancée, Page. I received a letter in the mail. It was from the University letting me know Pancho's ashes were ready to be returned. When I inquired, I had been told it could be as long as two years. I called and left a message. After a few days of playing phone tag, I was told his ashes would be overnighted. They would arrive on the Thursday before the wedding. They had chosen to have the wedding on Pancho's birthday June 22. He would be home for his birthday. He would be home for the wedding. I wondered how I would feel when they arrived. I had wondered if they would just show up one day.

I was waiting expectantly. All day I waited, working at one small task, then another, kind of walking in my circle dance when I heard the mail truck pull up and stop. I walked directly to the truck and in a matter of fact way I said, "You have my husband's ashes," signing the sheet he presented them to me. He looked shocked, how had he missed that fact, delivering mail every day for almost two years. I took the box in my arms and walked inside observing my emotions and surprised I did not cry. *What do I do with them? Where should he be for the wedding party?* I asked myself.

A few days earlier cleaning out the shed, I found a wonderful wooden box housing the compass from the Eyrie, his father's 32' Westsail. His ashes were in a cardboard box and they looked like a package. I decided to wrap the box in gift-wrap paper, paper with deer in a forest, wildlife, and other things Pancho loved. The wrapped package, gingerly placed atop a polished wooden pedestal, was displayed in the center of our living room shelf above the fireplace.

The same day while cleaning a closet I found one of my very favorite pictures, a black and white I had taken. It was a picture of Pancho mending a broken clue on the sail. It had been blown out by the stiff wind. He was sitting on the deck of the Odyssey Barge one foggy day moored in Falmouth, England in 1981. He had a full beard and was in his oilskins.

Next, I found a letter written to Pancho just before he died. It was from Pat. He was the captain of the sailboat we had lived on in Cornwall in 1982. He was writing, but did not know if Pancho was still alive. He wrote, "If Pancho is still with us, tell him to

183

put on his oilskins, he's wanted up on deck because it's his turn at the wheel." I printed the quote and placed it and the photograph with Pancho's ashes.

It was beautiful, it was *him*. I was so happy he came home at a time when we all needed him to let us know he was aware of our happy event planned for his birthday. My Skype account reminded me it was his birthday. It popped up with his picture. If he had lived, he would have been 63.

That was not the only sign he brought. On the day of the wedding, all was typically chaotic. I had a sign that needed to be put up near the beach at Marineland where they had chosen to be married. Lissa and I hurriedly took the sign indicating the area of Marineland parking lot where the guests should park. I had a hammer and a balloon to tie on the sign "Andersen Wedding" with an arrow.

I was vigorously pounding on the spike when Lissa noted, "Listen to those birds. What are they? Are they crows?" I heard the loud screeching and turned my attention to the sound. "No." I said as I looked up, "It's parrots!" Wild parrots! I exclaimed as we watched five green parrots fly overhead, one of Pancho's consistent signs.

I had heard of the parrots that had escaped from Marineland and bred in the area but never had I seen them. I took a deep breath. "Calm down, Shannon," I heard him say inside my head. I smiled, slowed down and just went with the flow even through the lightning storm, forgotten flowers, and the rings that never turned up for the ceremony.

One nice part of the processional was that there was a plan for the groomsmen to carry red roses, one of Pancho's first signs from the river on the day he died. They were each going to present them to me in memory of Pancho, on the empty chair beside me.

However, the roses were used for the bridesmaids and bride instead and they looked beautiful. Pancho's long board was a part of the altar made of bamboo. The bridesmaids' umbrellas provided an enchanting prop for the photos. The reception was full of joy, music, amazing food, and drink. It was full of laughter, fireworks, and mud! The bride and many of the bridal party jumped into the Intracoastal Waterway after posing for pictures including one with Page lifted above their heads on Pancho's longboard.

Page chose the Aerosmith song so special to me, "I Don't Want to Miss a Thing" for Treve and me to dance to. Even Pancho would have loved the wedding though he would have probably escaped upstairs long before the evening was over.

Reconciliation: I had certainly made it through all the previous stages Alan Wolfelt outlined. I had embraced the reality that Pancho was not coming back; he was dead. I had experienced the pain of the loss. I had certainly had my spiritual questioning going back to my knees to explore my beliefs; I had surrounded myself with the supporters who understood the necessity of grief and encouraged me to mourn long after the death.

At this stage, I began looking back at my pictures, ones I could not bear to look at before. I made a slide show of all of Pancho's pictures from the last year of his life. Should I keep the ones when he looked so bad? I no longer remembered him that way, his skin pulled so tight over his bones, not the least bit of a wrinkle, sharp edges. He did not look like the beautiful man I had always known but his eyes were Pancho. The pictures of Melissa putting cold clothes on his head, Treve and Dean massaging his feet and Lissa giving him a neck massage were too precious to release into never land with a click.

They were an important part of the journey leading up to his last breath and birth into the bigger reality. Putting those pictures together set me back a bit and I felt a true sadness but it came with the letdown after all the planning and time leading up to the wedding. I had no more uncontrollable bouts of crying, only the grief tears that streamed down my cheeks and dried quickly.

Writing had been put on the back burner when returning from Peru. I thought Peru was the last chapter but realized during the process of recording my story, it had its own time schedule and events to unfold. If in fact, I had a partner in this enterprise, then it would go places I could not anticipate.

When I had asked at Machu Picchu if Peru was the last chapter, I had received a "No." I had felt relieved, not yet ready to move on, tie the last knot in loose ends and end the chapter of my life with Pancho. Yet my old life and goals, my old passions and dreams began to tug distantly at my attention. The Templar book I had been working on for years, Molly's stories, all waiting for my energy, my Sacred Escapes tours and workshops had all been put on hold.

The pattern I had entered as I circled above my life was one I had desired, turning my day and life over. I had been invited to speak at a conference on *The Magdalene Awakening* in October. I was opening up to that next chapter, I just did not know the title. "Me, and the rest of my Life?" As always, I paid attention to the synchronicities and the master numbers of which I had written in my first book. They were a part of my connection to the beyond.

Beth and I took a trip to Daufuskie Island off the Georgia/South Carolina Coast for her birthday and enjoyed the beach. Pancho felt present in the herd of deer on the golf course and the beach. It was like the coastal island he loved to hunt. We watched the sunrises every morning and I glanced at the time when we arrived the first day, 6:22. I captured the picture. Pine trees, wildlife, sunrises, and full moon rises, were all reminders of Pancho. The children were thinking of him too.

I had brought a tiny bit of his ashes because Melissa asked to take some to Nicaragua. She was going to help with Finn, for the honeymoon. They were leaving the evening of the day Beth and I drove north and sent me a picture of a rainbow they saw on the way to the airport.

Their experience with signs from Pancho was quite profound. After releasing his ashes to the wind, Melissa sat crossed legged on the beach, alone, with her eyes closed. She was obviously sending the "I want to be alone signal" but never the less a surfer approached her. "Do you have the time? He asked. She picked up her phone. 6:22 she smiled. They also found a monkey at a restaurant named Pancho. I put a few of his ashes in the ocean in South Carolina and wondered what their ceremony was like.

When Beth and I arrived home, we vowed to enjoy our own beach. I met a woman on horseback and wanted to write her number down in my phone. I proceeded to do that and noticed it was 2:22. "Oh!" I said, "Let me show you something." I showed her my phone, adding, "I need to give you my book." "Oh, I see that number all the time." she said. We continued to talk and she asked, "Are you single?" "Single?" I responded, "Hum, I never thought of myself as single." I went on to explain I was a widow of 20 months

Single was a term that I guess I had to include in that next chapter. How was that going to feel?

Chapter Thirty-Seven
Reconciliation: Tying up a few loose ends.

How long does it take to reach reconciliation, the final stage of grief? It has been two years, two months and two days since Pancho died. I dreamt of my dead loved ones' last night. When I woke, I realized it was an important dream. I reached for my cell phone and began to record before the memories slipped away.

As I spoke into the microphone, describing the images, recording the faces and significant acts from my previous night's dreams, I realized Pancho was not there in any of the dreams. My Dad was. My brother, who was smiling and gave me a hug and a kiss, was. My nieces, sister, and a whole crowd of living family members were in my dream, but no Pancho. That has to be a portal, an initiation place in the road of grief.

For the months following my return from Peru I delved into the higher questions again. I studied philosophers and ideas. What was death? Were any of my beliefs valid? Were my little "t" truths reality?

With my computer on my lap, I turned on my new, fingertip to the ideas of others, YouTube, and watched for hours, shamans, and teachers, from Carl Jung and his *Red Book* to Terrence McKenna who studied the path of Amazonian botanical giving rise to the teachers from cultures long forgotten and to a portal to tomorrow.

Before Pancho died it was easy to rest on the soft bed of what I thought was true. There was no such thing as time…What we see as reality is but an illusion of light…We are not our bodies and whatever energy that is our consciousness continues…All ideas I had found comforting, that sustained me.

A great Universal Energy swirled in and around me. God, Wakan Tanka, the great mystery, available through prayer and always present, provided the guidance necessary for living. However, to those understandings over the months following what I thought would be the last chapter I overlaid what Terrence McKenna called Novelty…new thought, higher vision and a respect for what is unknowable.

Oh Valentine's Day 2015, it had been two years and three months since Pancho died and I came once again on a road mark of remembrance. I pulled the computer out and read the unedited chapter, which I had written one year before in Montana. It had been 41 years since our first Valentine's Day.

I thought back on the time when I first started working professionally exclusively with grief. At the time, I was amazed by the stories of the long relationships ended by death, the happy lives, and enduring love. Love stories poured out of the mouths of my clients.

What was I doing wrong? It was a period in our life when we were raising teenagers, working long hours and multiple jobs. Could I really have missed the boat? Was there a soul mate I had failed to find? Was there another half I had not found, as my clients were describing? Was there a perfect and compatible mate who synced up so closely that you breathed together, still held hands, and longed to touch at the end of each workday in the world?

What I discovered later was the stories remembered and retold after the loss of a loved one were usually the good memories. A grief story wasn't a biography of complete truths; it was a sorting of ideas, an attempt to validate the choices that brought one person together with another to walk the walk of life for a period of time, a big chunk of time. The stories I heard were unique, in that I entered the field of grief counseling the last third of my career and my clients who were at the time in their 70s and 80s were survivors of the WW II era. That was a devastating yet a romantic time to live. It was a time when love did not have to wait and people were brought together in a shared passion for each other through the reality of potential loss and separation.

After spending an extended time in grief counseling, my clients would loosen up and share the other parts of their long-term relationship. All of the stories were romantic to me. They helped me to have an entirely new perspective on my own long-term relationship and of course, only four years after starting my job with hospice Pancho's cancer diagnosis threw a new light on time, life, reality, and appreciation.

So I re-read the chapter I had written in Montana the previous Valentine Day, the one that launched my writing with a passion and I evaluated my journey. I had come a long, long way. I had started to melt the ice that held me inside my world. I went out dancing with a friend, received a hand drawn valentine from another, a box of candy from my grandson, Finn, and son, Treve, and a rose on Pancho's rose bush, just like last year.

The evening of Valentine's Day, I sat in front of the TV and there it was, the Betty White movie I had seen the year before. It was a wink from Pancho to go along with the rose bud blooming on the bush again. Yes, I think it was. That is what I would have to settle for, our own different form of a continuing, yet changing relationship. I know I will always love Pancho but I guess it is okay to begin to let go.

Chapter Thirty-Eight
How it works: Rainbows, Songs, and
Messages from Pancho

As the third anniversary of Pancho's death approached, I sat at my desk typing on my laptop. August 3, 2015: It was a week of initiation and release. My text chimed in at 6:54am from Treve fishing on the dock: Major Rainbow!

I jumped up from my computer where I had just completed the epilogue of my book. I hustled downstairs in my bathrobe and bare feet. I clicked my phone into camera mode. I began shooting pictures while pushing through the French doors afraid I would miss it any moment.

There was nothing to fear as it painted itself across the sky creating a dome over my house and dock for long minutes. I was able to take a video, while smiling and exclaiming the entire time. I posted a picture on Facebook, *Mother Nature's treasure,* and realized I had not even thought of giving Pancho the credit. I was making the transition to the next chapter.

I sat down on the dock to let it rain down on me for as long as it lasted, I thought about the Leslie Gore song "Sunshine, Lollypops and Rainbows." I pressed the Pandora App on my phone and it spontaneously began to play No Doubt's song, *Don't Speak*. A pain clinched my heart.

I had listened to it repeatedly after the death of Melissa's boyfriend, 14 years earlier. Listening brought up sadness and yet in some ways it comforted my grief. His death was a grief that had affected my life and I had survived. I wondered about the lyrics and brought them up on my phone:

You and me, we used to be together
Everyday together, always
I really feel that I'm losing my best friend
I can't believe this could be the end....
It looks as though you're letting go....
Don't tell me 'cause it hurts...
Our memories, they can be inviting
But some are altogether mighty frightening
As we die, both you and I

Don't tell me 'cause it hurts...
It's all ending...
I know you're good...
I know you're real good...
Oh...
Hush, hush darling...
Don't tell me 'cause it hurts...

"Darling." That is what Pancho called me but it sounded more like *darlin*. I felt sadness settle over me. I had not cried in so long, but now tears streamed down my face. Was he sad that I was starting to move forward? I did not believe that really, but I was sad, I wished I never had to let go.

I looked down at the next song popping up on Pandora. It was Aerosmith, but not "our song" - "I Don't Want to Miss a Thing". It was, "Dream On."

The past is gone
It went by, like dusk to dawn
Isn't that the way
Everybody's got the dues in life to pay...
Sing with me, just for today
Maybe tomorrow, the good Lord will take you away...
Dreams until your dreams come true...

And that is how this different form of continuing relationship works... That message felt better...it felt very real!

Chapter Thirty-Nine
Third Anniversary: Trying to Draw the Line in the Sand

I kept drawing a line in the sand and then finding I had to erase it and move it out a little farther! I do not want my experience to make the process seem so difficult. The entire journey was and is soulful. My grief was complicated by what I realized years of unresolved trauma had taken on and stored away.

The trauma was not only from walking beside Pancho on his march toward death, it was also from all the stories I heard every day as a counselor dealing was traumatic loss. My grief had extenuating circumstance and complex layers I had to deal with when I was finally forced to stop and do that. It was only then and reluctantly that I allowed myself. As I said, my mentor Alan Wolfelt, called the final stage of grief reconciliation.

In his book, *Journey through Grief*, Alan counseled:

"You may have heard it said, indeed, you may even believe that your grief journey's end will come when you resolve or recover from your grief. But your journey will never end. People do not "get over" grief. Reconciliation is a term I find more appropriate for integrating the new reality of moving forward in life, without the physical presence of the person who

died. With reconciliation comes a renewed sense of energy and confidence, and ability to fully acknowledge the reality of the death, and a capacity to become re-involved in the activities of living. In reconciliation, the sharp, ever-present pain of grief gives rise to a renewed sense of meaning and purpose. Your feeling of loss will not completely disappear, yet it will soften, and the intense pangs of grief will become less frequent. Hope for a continued life will emerge, as you are able to make commitments to the future. And realizing the person who died will never be forgotten yet knowing your life can move forward, will surface as your ability to heal."

Elizabeth Kubler-Ross called the final stage of grief, "Acceptance," but before acceptance comes sadness and along with sadness comes tears. Grief tears, I have been told are the kind that stream down your cheeks. They produce needed endorphins to help you heal.

I had gotten back into the swing of my life in the fall of 2015. I took a client on a personal Sacred Escape tour of Anglesey Island and the rest of Wales. I spent a week with Melissa in England. We returned home around the same time for another wedding, one of her best friends. Once more, I came home and once more, I had to readjust to being there. But during those months, my house was full of family and the baby as well as a houseguest.

I did not have much time to think, or write or grieve though I began to feel the storm clouds of the anniversary moving in again. When Melissa left for Norway in October and my houseguest left a couple of weeks later I found myself very alone for the first time in a very long time. The family compound seemed silent even though I kept the baby about 3 days a week and worked part time. Being alone was a challenge for me and I could feel the approaching anniversary. What would I do?

The day before Melissa flew back to Norway, we did a final internment. It was time to face Pancho's ashes and the marker that had been placed long ago. It had taken 3 years to gather the courage to bring Pancho's ashes to the Green lawn cemetery in Jacksonville. Our site is in the Garden of the Cross, near the remains and memories of many members of my family…. and friends…. It is beneath a beautiful oak tree and a place Pancho would have enjoyed sitting any day of the week.

Melissa accompanied me to make this final measure to bury some of Pancho's ashes at this marker of remembrance. Perhaps it is the women's place to grieve openly. Funny, like many people, I love cemeteries. This plot in the Garden of the Cross provides a place to come and remember Pancho and his life. I think he would have liked the marker with the surfer and our motto reminding us "Don't postpone your Joy" that we used as an affirmation the last years of his life.

I wrote this to say to the intimate group gathered that day:

You reach a place in your life when death becomes more common than not
When it is expected, and no longer feared and at times even welcomed
When we're young and no one in our life has died we

198

believe we will live forever and we can hold fairy tale
visions of fluffy clouds at the feet of Jesus
But life carries us down the river of reality
Which often turns into the river of sticks
Dark and murky we bounce from one bank to the
other
We are pushed forward by the tide until we learn to
turn the sticks to paddles
and then into oars and then we learn to push our boat
to the shore and learn to make a sail
and then perhaps we build or buy a motor with which
we can get around
the rocks as we move down the river of life
And, if we are lucky we find a Pilot to take the helm
who knows exactly where the river is to lead and the
water becomes clearer
and the bow begins to shimmer in the light of truth
We continue to move in the direction that we are
forever flowing, the direction of death
The direction of life that never ends but isn't the fairy
tale
The direction of unknowing
The direction in which the curtain will pull aside to
allow our boat to move through
But for now we are still in the river of life, which is
often tainted by the
tannin from the leaves, when the rains fall too hard
Then clears...we are still in the river sometimes
rolling and sometimes smooth
A river with a personality that we call life
We know there is a Pilot at the back of each of our
boats and we are reminded that soon, way too soon
we will follow Pancho through the veil that will part
for us and then all that is unknown will be known
And then all our questions will be answered
Then and only then...

Barry, my sister's former husband, and his wife, Lynn, and my sister, daughter, and Mother were there. Just after Pancho's death Barry had an incredible experience. He shared it at the memorial that day. He saw it was 2:22 and stepped out on his front porch just in time to see a gold star balloon floating by, just in front on him. His wife, Lynn, said "catch it" and Barry said, "Oh no! That's a sign from Pancho and he would never want to be caught."

The balloon floated up into the sky and disappeared. The next day they found a silver balloon in their backyard. I asked Barry to tell the story at the memorial that day, I had brought a silver and a gold balloon for Finn our only grandson to release, and in that, he took delight.

So that day I laid flowers on the marker left to remember Pancho, (flowers from our yard, lilies from the memorial plants we'd planted, roses, and ginger, firecracker plants and azaleas) all plants Pancho loved and nurtured.

The third anniversary came….and went. I had wanted to do something very special, like fly the remainder of his ashes to Nova Scotia to spread in the woods and on the beaches he loved, but it did not work out. I thought and thought, maybe I could finish the first draft of this book. What better way to remember Pancho than walking back through our lives together and looking once again at where I was and how far I'd come.

I remembered his words to me, "You just need to sit down and listen." Slow down, stop running, allow yourself to be with whatever you were feeling instead of trying to escape. So that is what I did. I was alone except for part of the day I spent with my grandson Finn.

Basically, the first draft was finished but it was not organized nor was it edited. Frankly, I wanted to hear it and see what I had completed during the three years I had worked on it sporadically, writing, and then going back months later to see what I had written. I, of course, wanted signs but I did not leave the house. During my morning journaling, when I checked in with all that I was feeling it was around 6:15 AM, I heard an owl. It was an audio journal and the sound of his hoot was picked up by my phone. I then looked at the clock, it was 6:22 AM.

I had often asked to see his name written. That happened, too. I noticed a little round flat rock, a tiny one sitting on the bookcase next to my bed and picked it up. On it was my handwriting .... *Pancho*. It was one of the rocks I found on the beach at Nerja, Spain and inscribed for Melissa to leave on the Camino. I truly just felt sad all day but I worked diligently reading aloud the chapters of this book and listening to myself read them.

The next morning my sister called and so did my son to check on me. I merged the calls and while we were talking about my experience, a bald eagle flew by. I sat by the river in the porch swing, and I checked in with myself. Inside my chest, it felt like no time had elapsed. For that moment I felt the same as I had the day Pancho died, empty.

There was a sadness in my heart. I remembered Pancho's admonition to sit and be still so I picked up my drum and for an hour, I closed my eyes and pounded. Like I had done on the Labyrinth at Chartres Cathedral, I mentally walked back through the past 3 years of my life and the tears flowed. I cried.

Was I ready to release? I spent the anniversary finishing first draft of this book, a journal of grief and remembrance for the man I loved. Thank you Pancho, I think you honored your promise and you did a really good job! I hope the waves are good in heaven and I think, I am almost sure.... I will be okay without you here. I will always love you.

Most likely, I will cry from time to time for the rest of my life. Grief never dies. It is always there, ready to be triggered. Tears remain as a tribute to love. I will have to rest with that. Pancho was not able to come and sit by me and tell me about death and what exists on the other side of life. He came to me through signs, and as I look back, I cannot dispute, they were too synchronistic to reject. He came to me through dreams where we could hold each other and cry and through angels in the form of people who helped me clean up all he left behind. And he came to me as people who helped me to tie up the loose ends of the chapter of 'us', and people to help me begin to write the chapter of 'me' and the rest of my life.

I had many analogies I used when I helped others in their grieving and they were all true. I had turned my headlights inward, like the cars that used to flip their lights into disappearance during the daytime and I focused on my insides. The light went out on the sun and it was cloudy every day for a long time. But, one day the sun came out again and I began to smile. I held hands, danced like an adolescent, and blushed at the attentions of men. I went through all the awkward questions about what I wanted for my future and sat in the unknown with all its discomforts. I began to the embrace the realization, *THAT* is the reality. The *unknown* is the truth. Ultimately, what I have is what Terrence McKenna calls, "true enough" as I gradually release Pancho to his next chapter, I will start writing mine.

I know I will never be the same but there is nothing that can bring Pancho back. He lives in my heart and in my thoughts and in the way I see the world. He lives in my children and my grandchild who now snuggles next to me on Pancho's side of the bed. That will have to do until the next time we meet.

Chapter Forty:
When Next We Meet

I know what it will be like the next time we meet. I had a vision at the Bighorn Medicine Wheel in Wyoming. The summer of 2011, Beth, Pancho, and I headed to Montana to Debbie and Fred's house. We wanted to explore the area. We especially wanted to visit the Bighorn Medicine Wheel in North Dakota. It was another one of Beth's' planned pilgrimage trips for which Pancho ended up being her stand-in.

We had planned the trip for years and had traveled thousands of miles to get there. We arrived at the Bighorn before noon on July 21, 2011. The first thing we encountered was a giant snow bank that covered the entire road at the park ranger station. The park rangers highly recommended that we not cross. Beth had been concerned about the altitude and the walk, and her health, but a snow bank was nothing we had ever considered as an obstacle.

Beth walked ahead swiftly. She beat us by yards. I began to follow her but my shoes were not appropriate for the snow. The ice was slippery and then there was a 2000 foot fall if you tripped. Beth turned around and started walking back crying, "I'm not going to do this." "Your knees will never do this!" she warned.

I started. I tried to walk but my knees would not do it! Holy Cow, we came all this way and we are not going to make it. About that time, Pancho arrived and stood at the base. "Oh no, not again," he said in dismay. We stood at the edge of the snow and Pancho was aghast, "You mean, you came all this way and you are not going to cross?"

Beth went over and sat down. My knee was really painful and uncooperative in terms of locking and flexibility. I, too, was afraid. If you looked down the white slope, there was nothing but a steep incline heading off into the forest at the bottom. "You guys are crazy." Pancho said and he started across.

"You go for us. Just take our stuff." I handed him my bag full of medal and my medicine bag that I had brought with me. I had a medicine bag I had been carrying with me for many years and cherished it more since I had learned of my Native-American roots. It held Hopi cornmeal and a genuine gemstone of every color of the chakras along with a variety of other treasures I had collected. At the very least, I wanted my medicine bag to go to the top.

Beth sat down a short distance from the path and I went to try to talk her into changing her mind. I mustered some courage of my own. Pancho disappeared out of sight with his long strides as he took on our mission. Just then, a woman at least 10 years older than me came walking across from the other direction using two ski poles as she maneuvered the groove of the slick worn path. "Man," I said to her, "Do you think I can make it?" "Sure" she said, "I'll help you get across." "You'd really do that?" "Yeah I'll do that."

I threw my purse back to Beth, put my phone in my pocket, and tried not to look down. I followed her one step at a time. It was terrifying but before I knew it, I had been guided across the snow bank and was on the other side. "Are you going to be okay?" she asked. "Yeah, my husband is over here" I replied.

Alone, I set out up the hill. I had no idea how far ahead Pancho was nor how long the walk to the top. The wind was blowing briskly in my ear. The view spread out over the South Dakota hills and I walked alone and thought. I thought about the metaphor of the walk. The experience was so poignant. I knew that inevitably one of us would be leaving the other. It would most likely be Pancho who was first called by death. I knew that one day I would follow. I thought about our life. As I kept looking off into the distance I thought about his leaving me, not just that day but really leaving me, dying. I was overcome with fear and I began to cry.

I had a vision of a time to come when we would meet again, not on that day but sometime in the future when I too would cross through the veil. I strained my eyes to see him and kept trudging upward, my heart beating in my ears as I hurried to reach the top. When I got to the top, there he was standing with his hands held up above his head waving.

And I thought, "This is what I want it to be like when I cross over, I want to imagine this moment at the top of the medicine wheel and there he'll be greeting me. I want it to look just like this."

206

Editor's Epilogue

Shannon originally entitled her book "Scream, Run, Cry". From this editor's view, it is a love story, a love story about Shannon's relationship with Pancho. And, it is not sad. Also, Shannon's experiences, the synchronicities described in her book, are multi-dimensional links in the parallel universes. The implications of Quantum Mechanics connect human consciousness with how the physical world reveals itself and what happens in it. What we think, what we expect, what we hold in our consciousness, even in our sub consciousness; does create reality. The power of thought creates an energy field that alters what happens in material reality.

"Parallel Universes" describes the Quantum Mechanical nature of their relationship. In Quantum Mechanical terms, her consciousness and his consciousness are separate parallel universes running alongside each other for eternity, never ending. Parallel lines never touch or intersect each other and yet there is communication. When one line resonates energetically with passion, the other line running along side resonates in sympathy. In the same way violin, piano, or guitar strings pick up vibration, synchronicities occur when nearby beings vibrate sympathetically. Their consciousness communicates energetically with synchronicities providing special meanings. Humans use words.

When Shannon sees rainbows or Master Numbers, she experiences communication. Not words, but symbols resonating from special experiences and relationships once shared and enjoyed. The meanings sent from a consciousness existing in a parallel universe communicates via synchronicities and coincidences and they express the shared meaning to the other waiting to receive. Meaningful coincidences and synchronicities used instead of words. How better else to communicate something not easily put into words? Many having near death experiences cannot find words to adequately explain their feelings and emotions. They had been somewhere words do not belong.

About the Author

L. Shannon Andersen, LMHC

Shannon Andersen is a writer and a Transpersonal Life Coach with a Masters in Mental Health Counseling and has practiced as a licensed counselor in Florida for over 25 years. From 1998-2012 she worked as a bereavement counselor for hospice where she focused on grief and has spent years of study in religion, psychology, metaphysics, and *A Course in Miracles*, applying the knowledge she gleaned to her writing and work as a Transpersonal Life Coach. She was trained by Dr. Brian Weiss author of "Many Lives, Many Masters" in past life regression therapy in 1996 and works with individuals seeking to explore their spiritual emergence. She is an international speaker doing workshops across the world. Her professional credentials include training in hypnosis,

NLP, EMDR, TFT, Traumatology and she is a Compassion Fatigue Specialist holding a certification in Critical Incident Stress Debriefing (CISM). Shannon loves working with doctors, nurses, counselors and other professionals to help them take care of themselves. Shannon took her accredited life coach training from the Institute of Life Coach Training created by Dr. Patrick Williams and now offers transpersonal life coaching to a limited number of clients. She has been published in "The Florida Journal of Public Health" and "Florida Living Magazine", and featured in a 2002 issue of "Q Magazine," a popular and trendy publication in Hong Kong. She is the author of *The Magdalene Awakening: Symbol and Synchronicity Heralding the Re-emergence of the Divine Feminine. Finding Elizabeth: True Stories of Comfort for Grieving Hearts* and was included in *The Cathar View: The Mysterious Legacy of Montsegur,* a compendium published by Polair Publishing in London, England. Among her short stories are a series called *Molly Tales Worth Telling* recounting the mysterious stories of Molly Worth who grew up in England as a part of the Great Generation. She does workshops and private retreats and takes people on personal tours of sacred sites. www.TheMagdaleneAwakening.com: Facebook L. Shannon Andersen and Sacred Escapes Retreat Center.